Indonesia

Indonesia

BY NEL YOMTOV

Enchantment of the World™
Second Series

CHILDREN'S PRESS®

An Imprint of Scholastic Inc.

New York   Toronto   London   Auckland   Sydney
Mexico City   New Delhi   Hong Kong
Danbury, Connecticut

Frontispiece: **Buddha statue, Borobudur**

Consultant: Andrea Molnar, Department of Anthropology, Northern Illinois University, Dekalb, Illinois

Please note: All statistics are as up-to-date as possible at the time of publication.

Book production by The Design Lab

Library of Congress Cataloging-in-Publication Data
Yomtov, Nelson.
  Indonesia / by Nel Yomtov.
      pages cm. — (Enchantment of the world)
  Includes bibliographical references and index.
  Audience: Grades 4–6.
  ISBN 978-0-531-21253-0 (library binding)
1. Indonesia—Juvenile literature. 2. Indonesia—History—Juvenile literature. 3. Indonesia—
Civilization—Juvenile literature. I. Title.
  DS615.Y66 2014
  959.8—dc23   2014031108

1 2 3 4 5 6 7 8 9 10 R 24 23 22 21 20 19 18 17 16 15

Tenun dancers

Contents

Left to right: **Rice farmer, Wayag Islands, children, monks at Borobudur, bicycle taxi**

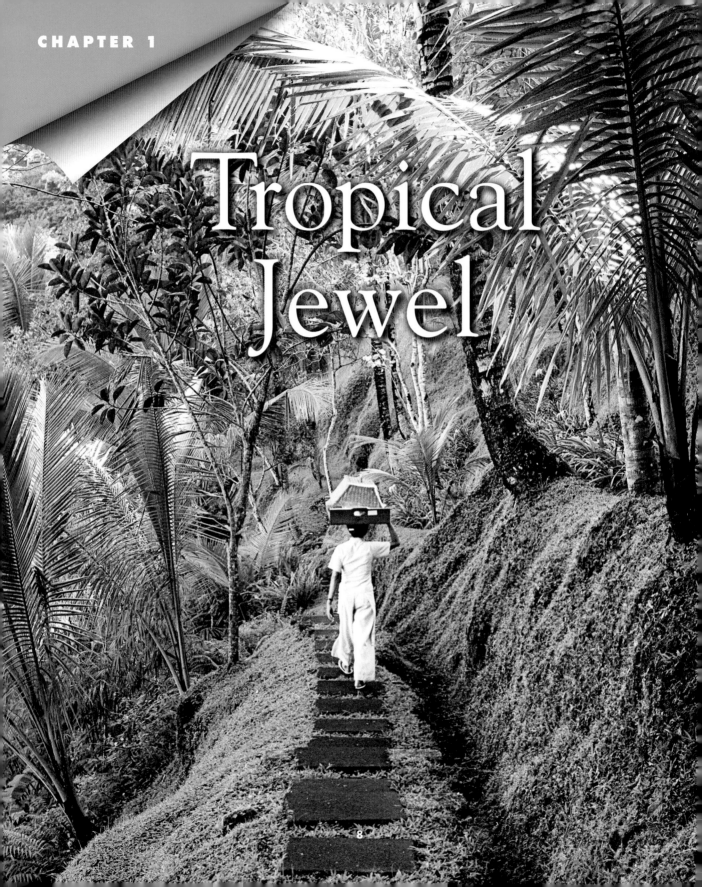

CHAPTER 1

Tropical Jewel

NICKNAMED THE EMERALD OF THE EQUATOR, THE nation of Indonesia is made up of 17,500 islands that stretch across the seas from the Indian Ocean to the Pacific Ocean. The islands feature a wide assortment of natural wonders. They boast lush rain forests, colorful wildlife, looming volcanoes, and immaculate beaches.

The island of Java is the heart of the nation. Java is home to Indonesia's capital city, Jakarta, and other bustling cities that are filled with high-rise buildings and clogged with traffic. It also features peaceful countryside and astounding cultural sites, such as the massive Buddhist temple Borobudur. Other islands are equally beautiful. Sumatra is a postcard-picture image of a tropical paradise. With near-constant rain, flowers and wildlife flourish in the island's forests, valleys, and mountains. Bali is small in size but offers plenty to enjoy, including pounding surf and spellbinding Hindu temple ceremonies.

Opposite: **A woman carries food baskets on her head through the lush forests of Bali.**

A woman buys produce at a floating market in South Kalimantan on the island of Borneo. Most people in this region are of the Banjarese ethnic group.

Indonesia is a diverse country. It is home to roughly 253 million people who belong to three hundred different ethnic groups and speak hundreds of different languages. But Indonesia's people are also united in many ways. In addition to their local language, they speak the national language, Indonesian. Eighty-seven percent of the population shares a common religion—Islam—but Indonesia is not an Islamic state. Christianity, Hinduism, Buddhism, and local religions are also practiced.

Indonesia's history is as diverse and captivating as its land and people. Early humans inhabited the islands more than one million years ago. Modern humans arrived in the islands some seventy thousand years ago. Eventually, hundreds of kingdoms developed throughout the islands. Traders from many parts of Asia, including India, Persia, Arabia, and China, traveled to Indonesia, adding new elements to the islands' already diverse mix of religions, arts, and cultures.

Black domes rise from the grand mosque in Banda Aceh, the capital of the Aceh province. The building is a mixture of Dutch and Middle Eastern architecture.

Europeans began to arrive in the region in the early 1500s. The Portuguese came first, in search of spices, followed by the Dutch, who ruled many of the islands—often brutally—for hundreds of years. In the early 1800s, the British took over many of these islands, but they later reverted to Dutch control. During World War II, Japan invaded Indonesia and seized power until the war's end. Finally, in 1945, after countless bloody battles with foreign intruders, Indonesia declared its independence.

Independence did not bring peace to the islands. Violence has erupted as some regions have tried to establish independent nations. From 1975 to 1988, Indonesian troops battled independence fighters in a region called East Timor, or Timor-Leste. Thousands of people were killed before Timor-Leste achieved its independence in 2002. Years of fighting between separatists in Aceh, in northern Sumatra, and government forces in Indonesia finally ended with a cease-fire agreement in 2005. An ongoing hot spot is Papua, an eastern region that only became fully integrated into Indonesia in 1969 following a vote among the Papuans that many people think was rigged. Indonesian troops and police have now battled Papuan separatist groups for decades.

Despite these troubles, many people believe the future looks bright for the Emerald of the Equator. With its abundant natural resources, well-educated workforce, and democratic government, Indonesia is poised to become a true paradise.

Workers construct a tower in downtown Jakarta. The city has dozens of skyscrapers that rise more than forty floors.

CHAPTER 2

A Nation of Islands

THE REPUBLIC OF INDONESIA OCCUPIES MOST OF the Malay Archipelago, the largest archipelago, or chain of islands, in the world. The nation's roughly 17,500 islands stretch over an area of 735,358 square miles (1,904,569 square kilometers), extending 3,200 miles (5,150 km) from east to west and 1,100 miles (1,770 km) from north to south. Indonesia is the fifteenth-largest country in the world, about three times the size of the U.S. state of Texas and one-fifth the size of the United States. The Indonesians refer to their homeland as *Tanah Air Kita*, which means "Our Nation of Land and Water."

Opposite: **Many of the thousands of islands in Indonesia are completely uninhabited, often because the islands have no fresh water.**

Land and Water

Ocean surrounds Indonesia. The Indian and Pacific Oceans border the western and eastern parts of the islands. Seas such as Andaman, Java, Banda, and Celebes separate island groups.

Indonesia's Geographic Features

Area: 735,358 square miles (1,904,569 sq km)

Highest Elevation: Jaya Peak, 16,024 feet (4,884 m) above sea level

Lowest Elevation: Sea level along the coast

Longest River: Kapuas (right), 710 miles (1,143 km)

Largest Lake: Lake Toba, 426 square miles (1,103 sq km)

Largest City (2014 est.): Jakarta, population 9,608,000

Average High Temperature: In Jakarta, 89°F (32°C)

Average Low Temperature: In Jakarta, 77°F (25°C)

Average Annual Rainfall: In Jakarta, 73 inches (185 cm)

Indonesia's islands vary tremendously. Of the vast number of these islands, 6,700 are inhabited. Sumatra is larger than the U.S. state of California, while Java is home to more people than any other island in the world. Many smaller islands feature little more than a few trees and plants. Some are so small that they do not even have a name.

The islands of Indonesia fall into four main groups: the Greater Sunda Islands, the Lesser Sunda Islands, the Maluku Islands, and New Guinea.

The Greater Sunda Islands consist of Sumatra, Java, Borneo, and Sulawesi. Most of the country's population lives on these islands. Approximately 50 million people, or 22 percent of Indonesia's total population, live on Sumatra. It is an island of dazzling beauty, home to steaming volcanoes, lush forests, and extensive white-sand beaches.

Java is roughly the size of North Carolina and is home to 143 million people, or nearly 57 percent of the nation's population. The island is a mix of mountains, eroded rocky land, and

Guides lead tourists on an elephant trek through Sumatra's thick forests. Sumatra was once covered with rain forest, but much of it has now been logged.

Killer Waves

It was a December Indonesians will always remember. On the morning of December 26, 2004, a magnitude 9.0 earthquake violently shook the seafloor 100 miles (160 km) off the west coast of Sumatra. The earthquake was caused by the shifting and sliding of tectonic plates, which make up the earth's outer layer. Heaving with the power of 23,000 atomic bombs, the quake unleashed a series of deadly tsunami waves that spread across the Indian Ocean at speeds of up to 500 miles per hour (805 kph). Within a few hours, killer waves as high as 50 feet (15 meters) crashed into coastal communities of eleven Indian Ocean nations, including Indonesia, Thailand, India, and Sri Lanka. The quake was the third largest in recorded history. It was so powerful that it caused the entire planet to vibrate roughly one-quarter of an inch (0.6 centimeters). The rumbling

also triggered smaller earthquakes as far off as the U.S. state of Alaska, nearly 7,000 miles (11,300 km) away.

The devastation was overwhelming. More than 160,000 people were killed in Sumatra alone, as towns and villages were swept away by the giant waves (above). An estimated 280,000 people were killed in fourteen countries, including roughly 220,000 in Indonesia. Nearly 200,000 more people were injured or missing, and close to 1.7 million people were made homeless by the tragedy.

People from around the world stepped forward to assist the victims of the disaster. Governments contributed billions of dollars, and private citizens donated millions more. Thousands of international volunteers flocked to the region to help. Through the efforts of Indonesians and people from around the world, the region has been rebuilt.

plains. Java's economy is the most developed in all of Indonesia, and it is the site of Jakarta, the island's capital and largest city.

Borneo is split between three nations: Indonesia, Malaysia, and Brunei. The Indonesian part of the island is called Kalimantan. Almost 15 million people live in Kalimantan. The logging and mining industries have diminished much of the island's natural beauty, but the interior still features towering mountains, thick forests, and mighty rivers.

Sulawesi is roughly the size of Great Britain. With a population of more than 18 million, it is Indonesia's third most

Clouds frequently hang over the mountains in Java.

Because Indonesia is a nation of islands, it has tens of thousands of miles of coastline and many beautiful beaches.

populous island. The island has an unusual shape, with four tentacle-like peninsulas. The interior of the island includes rugged mountainous terrain and deep valleys. Several active volcanoes are found in the northern Minahassa Peninsula.

The Lesser Sunda Islands stretch to the east of the Greater Sunda Islands. Hundreds of islands make up the Lesser Sunda Islands. The largest are Lombok and Sumbawa in the west, and Flores, Sumba, and Timor in the east. To the west of the group is Bali, the country's most popular tourist destination, with remarkable white- and black-sand beaches, colorful coral reefs, and vibrant culture. The island of Timor is divided. The western half is part of Indonesia. The eastern half declared its independence from Indonesia in 1999 and is now the independent nation of Timor-Leste.

The Maluku Islands lie in the northeastern part of Indonesia. In earlier times, the Malukus were often called the

Looking at Indonesia's Cities

Jakarta, the capital of Indonesia, is also its largest city, with a population of about 10,188,000. The second-largest city, with a population of about 3,010,000, is Surabaya (right), the capital of the province of East Java. The earliest accounts of the city appear in a book written by a Chinese government official in 1255. Surabaya developed into a major trading center, and today it is one of Indonesia's busiest ports. The 17,841-foot-long (5,440 m) Suramadu Bridge is the longest in the country and the first bridge to cross the Madura Strait, connecting the islands of Java and Madura. Its completion spurred economic growth in the region. Other points of interest include the Al-Akbar Mosque and the Mpu Tantular Museum, which features a large collection of ancient Javanese art, weapons, pottery, and coins.

With an estimated population of 2,560,000 people, Bandung, the capital of the province of West Java, is Indonesia's third-largest city. Situated 2,520 feet (770 m) above sea level, Bandung has a cooler climate than most Indonesian cities. Bandung's economy is based mainly on tourism, textiles, agriculture, technology, and financial services. With nearly fifty institutions of higher learning, the city is one of Indonesia's most important centers for education. Bandung is home to fine examples of Dutch colonial architecture, many which feature traditional Indonesian themes and design.

Medan (left), the capital of the North Sumatra province, is Indonesia's fourth-largest city, with a population of 2,242,000. The city began to flourish after the 1860s, when Dutch colonists established tobacco plantations in the region. Within a few decades, Medan blossomed into an important center for government and commerce. Maimun Palace is one of the city's landmarks. Built in the late nineteenth century by Sultan Makmun Al Rasyid Perkasa Alamsyah, the palace incorporates diverse architectural elements, including Malay, Muslim, Indian, Spanish, and Italian styles.

Spice Islands because the cloves, nutmeg, and other spices that attracted traders from distant lands were grown there. The Malukus number more than one thousand. The largest islands in the chain are Halmahera, Seram, and Buru. Slightly more than two million people live in the Malukus, or less than 1 percent of Indonesia's population.

The final piece in the Indonesian archipelago is the island of New Guinea. The western half of the island is part of Indonesia and includes two Indonesian provinces, Papua and West Papua. The eastern half of New Guinea is the independent country of Papua New Guinea. Snowcapped mountains, rain forests, wetlands, and grasslands dominate the island. Jaya Peak, the highest mountain in Indonesia at 16,024 feet (4,884 meters), is in Papua.

Wasur National Park includes part of the largest wetland in Papua. The park features many kinds of landscapes, including swamp forests, grasslands, and bamboo forests, and provides habitat for more than 350 kinds of birds.

Mountains and Volcanoes

Mountains and volcanoes are the dominant physical features of most Indonesian islands. A central mountain range runs the length of the entire Indonesian archipelago. Large, rugged mountains are found on Sumatra, Java, Bali, Lombok, Sulawesi, Seram, New Guinea, Flores, Timor, and throughout the Maluku Islands. Major Indonesian mountain ranges include the Barisan Mountains, which run along the western edge of Sumatra, and the Maoke Mountains, in New Guinea.

Indonesia lies on the Ring of Fire, a horseshoe-shaped line of volcanoes around the edge of the Pacific Ocean. Indonesia has more than one hundred active volcanoes, the most of any nation in the world. Krakatoa, which lies in the Sunda Strait between Sumatra and Java, erupted disastrously in 1883. The most active volcanoes today are Merapi and Kelud on Java. As recently as October 2010, more than 350 people were killed during eruptions of Mount Merapi. Several villages

Mount Merapi rises 9,610 feet (2,930 m) in central Java. The volcano has erupted frequently during the last five hundred years.

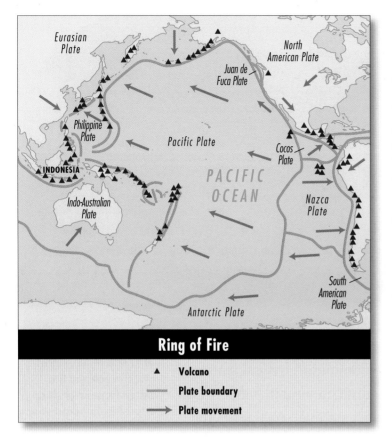

Eurasian Plate

North American Plate

Juan de Fuca Plate

Philippine Plate

Pacific Plate

INDONESIA

Cocos Plate

PACIFIC OCEAN

Indo-Australian Plate

Nazca Plate

South American Plate

Antarctic Plate

Ring of Fire

▲ Volcano

Plate boundary

Plate movement

were destroyed and hundreds of thousands of people were evacuated from their homes. In February 2014, Mount Kelud erupted, destroying or damaging more than 12,000 buildings. The volcanic ash spewed by the volcano prompted more than 75,000 residents to evacuate villages.

Lakes and Rivers

Indonesia has roughly 520 natural lakes. The largest lake in the country is Lake Toba in northern Sumatra. It formed in the crater of a volcano following an eruption more than seventy thousand years ago. Toba is the largest volcanic lake in the world, measuring 62 miles (100 km) at its maximum length and 19 miles (30 km) at its maximum width. With an average depth of roughly 1,640 feet (500 m), it is also one of the world's deepest lakes. On the north side of the lake is a 400-foot (120 m) waterfall called Sipiso-piso, which means "like a knife."

The largest river in Indonesia is the Kapuas in West Kalimantan on the island of Borneo. At 710 miles (1,143 km) long, it connects the interior of the island with its western coast. The Kapuas is wide and deep enough to be used for

The Day the World Exploded

On August 26 and 27, 1883, a series of four titanic explosions rocked the island of Krakatoa (right), located between Java and Sumatra. Over a five-hour period, powerful volcanic eruptions destroyed three-quarters of the island, and other islands nearby. The 2,600-foot-high (793 m) volcanic mountain was blasted completely away. All that remained was a 1,000-foot-deep (305 m) hole in the ocean floor. Rock and debris from the mountain was hurled more than 17 miles (27 km) into the atmosphere. The roars of the blasts were heard more than 2,200 miles (3,540 km) away in Australia.

The eruption devastated the region. On Java and Sumatra alone, more than thirty-six thousand people were killed and 165 villages were destroyed. Thousands of people were killed in lava flows. Some of the lava flows, capable of reaching temperatures of up to 1,800 degrees Fahrenheit (1,000 degrees Celsius),

traveled across the waters on a cushion of steam all the way to Sumatra—more than 25 miles away (40 km)! Huge tsunami waves produced by the eruption stretched out across the surrounding seas, sinking ships as far away as India and South Africa. Some estimates place the eruption's total death toll at 120,000.

For nearly three days after the eruption, a thick black cloud of dust and ash hung over the region. As winds carried the ash and other volcanic material in the atmosphere around the world, weather patterns changed. Summer temperatures in the Northern Hemisphere dropped by as much as 2.2°F (1.2°C). Record rainfall in California in the year following the eruption has been credited to the monstrous blasts. The fine dust spewed into the atmosphere darkened the sky worldwide and caused spectacular sunsets for more than three years.

Today, the volcano is rebuilding itself as lava seeps out through crevices in the ground and hardens. Since the 1950s, it has grown about 5 inches (13 cm) taller per week, and now stands 620 feet (189 m) above sea level. The new mountain is called Anak Krakatau (left), or Child of Krakatoa.

Changing Colors

The island of Flores contains one of Indonesia's most unique geographic features: the dormant volcano Kelimutu, which has not one but three dazzling crater lakes. Rocky ridges separate the lakes from one another. But what is truly astounding is that each lake has its own distinct color. Tiwu Ata Bupu (Lake of Old People) is usually blue. Tiwu Ko' Fai Nuwa Muri (Lake of Young Men and Maidens) is usually bright turquoise, while Tiwu Ata Polo (Lake of the Witches) is often bright red or burgundy. Sometimes, unpredictably, the lakes change colors. Scientists believe the different colors are the result of chemical reactions as different gases are emitted from the volcano below.

shipping. During seasons of heavy rainfall, the river overflows its banks. Much of the overflow is diverted to a system of nearby lakes. The outflow of water assists fish migrating from the river to the lakes to spawn, or lay eggs. It also prevents flooding at inhabited areas at the lower end of the river.

Climate

Indonesia is located on the equator, an imaginary line that runs around the globe halfway between the North and the South Poles. Indonesia is also surrounded by warm ocean waters. These two factors contribute to the nation having a hot and humid tropical climate. On average, the temperature in Jakarta reaches a daytime high of 89°F (32°C) throughout the year. Mountainous regions are cooler. It even snows sometimes in the Maoke Mountains.

The wet season in Indonesia generally lasts from December to March. During these months, heavy downpours sometimes cause major flooding. June to September are the driest months. Mountainous regions receive the most rain. In some areas 240 inches (610 cm) fall every year. The Lesser Sunda Islands that are closest to Australia generally receive the least rain, averaging 40 to 60 inches (100 to 150 cm) per year.

Indonesians wade through floodwaters in Jakarta. The city often suffers flooding during the rainy season.

CHAPTER 3

Wildlife Treasures

NDONESIA BOASTS A DAZZLING VARIETY OF ANIMAL and plant life. Hundreds of thousands of different species of plants and animals live in the diverse ecosystems found in Indonesia. It is estimated that Indonesia is home to 12 percent of the world's mammal species, 16 percent of the world's amphibian and reptile species, and 17 percent of the world's bird species. Many amazing creatures can be found only in Indonesia.

Opposite: **A young orangutan clings to its mother in a forest on Sumatra. Orangutans live only on Sumatra and Borneo.**

The Wallace Line

From 1854 to 1862, British explorer and naturalist Sir Alfred Russel Wallace traveled throughout the islands of Indonesia. His goal was to gather wildlife specimens to study and sell to museums. By the end of his journey, Wallace had collected more than 126,000 types of flora and fauna. He published his findings in a book called *The Malay Archipelago*.

Studying his vast collection, Wallace realized that the Indonesian archipelago had two separate zones of different plants

A babirusa's tusks continue to grow throughout its life. They curve backward and sometimes actually pierce the animal's skull.

and animals. The dividing line, known as the Wallace Line, runs between Borneo and Sulawesi, and through the Lombok Strait between Bali and Lombok. On the west side of the line, the wildlife resembles that found in Asia. On the east side, it is similar to the nature of Australia. On some islands, including Maluku and Sulawesi, both types of wildlife can be found.

Mammals

The one-horned Javan rhinoceros is one of the most endangered species in the world. The total known world population of forty individuals lives in Ujung Kulon National Park at the western tip of Java. The babirusa, a type of pig, has long tusks that grow into its upper lip. Two types of anoas, or dwarf buffalo, live in the forests of Sulawesi. Anoas look like a cross between a deer and a cow.

Indonesia is also home to many varieties of primates. Two endangered species of orangutan—the Bornean and the Sumatran—live only on those islands. Another primate, the proboscis monkey, lives only on Borneo. It is easily identifiable because of its unusually large nose, which hangs lower than its mouth. Gibbons and siamangs live on Sumatra, while Sulawesi is home to several species of macaques as well as tarsiers, small, short-haired, goggle-eyed primates that leap through the forest from tree trunk to tree trunk.

Another striking wildlife creature in Indonesia is the lesser mouse deer, the world's smallest known hoofed animal. It stands only 18 inches (46 cm) high and weighs only 4.4

A lesser mouse deer feeds on the forest floor next to a partridge. This small mammal eats leaves, buds, and fruit that has fallen to the ground.

pounds (2 kilograms), and lives in thickly wooded forests. The eastern islands are also home to marsupials such as tree-climbing kangaroos and bandicoots, which are medium-sized creatures about the size of rabbits, with pointy snouts, humped backs, and large hind feet. The odd-looking pangolin, sometimes called the scaly anteater, is covered in tough leatherlike scales. They burrow into the ground in search of ants and termites that they capture with their long, sticky tongue. When frightened or in danger, the pangolin quickly rolls itself up into a tight ball, and is protected by its scales.

Bird Life

More than 1,500 species of birds live in Indonesia. Bird species include the snow-white feathered Bali myna. The tips of its wings and tail are black, and its eyes are surrounded by blue bare skin. The Javan plover lives along wetlands and sandy shores and beaches. Many types of hornbills are found in Indonesia.

National Bird

The Javan hawk-eagle is the national bird of Indonesia. It is commonly called the Garuda, after a birdlike creature in Buddhist and Hindu stories. The Javan hawk-eagle is one of the world's rarest raptors—birds that hunt other animals. Only about 325 pairs of Javan hawk-eagles live in the wild.

These birds, which have large, curved bills, feature in the traditional stories of many Indonesian ethnic groups.

The cerulean paradise flycatcher, with its bright blue feathers and bluish-black beak, lives only on the island of Sangihe, off northern Sulawesi. The bird was thought to be extinct until several were found in 1998. Maluku and Papua are home to the cassowary, a large flightless black bird and one of the heaviest birds on earth. Adults can weigh as much as 155 pounds (70 kg). Maleos live in tropical lowlands and hill forests on Sulawesi. They make their nests in open beach areas or in volcanic soils that are warmed by the sun or heat from within the earth.

Reptiles

Roughly seventy species of reptiles are found only in Indonesia. One of the most unusual is the Malayan gharial, a freshwater crocodile with a thin, long snout. In the wild, male gharials can grow to 16 feet (5 m) long and weigh as much as 550 pounds (250 kg). Adults feed on proboscis monkeys, deer, waterbirds, and macaques. The Bornean earless monitor lizard was first discovered in 1877. Despite its name, it can hear, although it does not have any visible signs of ears. Snakes in

Cassowaries can grow more than 6 feet (2 m) tall, which is as tall as an adult man. They can run quickly, reaching 30 miles (50 km) per hour.

Indonesia include the venomous coral snake, the king cobra, the banded krait, and varieties of vipers. Indonesia is also home to the reticulated python, the longest snake species in the world. The longest reticulated python ever found was nearly 33 feet (10 m) long.

Turtle species in Indonesia include the Roti Island snake-necked turtle, which lives on Rote Island near Timor. Nearly extinct, this turtle is a favorite among pet owners around the world. Since 2001, it has been illegal to collect this species, although its numbers continue to dwindle. Two types of large river turtles, the mangrove terrapin and the painted terrapin, live in creeks and rivers. Both are critically endangered

It takes five people to hold up a 20-foot-long (6 m) reticulated python. Some pythons this size weigh 300 pounds (135 kg).

Indonesia is home to the world's largest lizard, the Komodo dragon. This remarkable creature lives on the archipelago's hot, dry volcanic islands. Komodo dragons can grow up to 10 feet (3 m) long and weigh 330 pounds (150 kg). These ferocious predators can move short distances quickly. They use their keen eyesight, sharp claws, and wide, powerful jaws to hunt and kill their prey, which includes other Komodo dragons. The bacteria in their saliva can cause infections, so even if the prey is not killed immediately when it is attacked, the bite often becomes infected and the prey eventually dies. Roughly 2,500 to 5,000 Komodo dragons remain in the wild. Most live in the Komodo National Park habitat on the islands of Komodo, Padar, Rinca, and a few other nearby islands.

because they are illegally hunted for pet food and human food, and because their habitat is being used for farms.

Sea Life

Roughly 25 percent of the world's fish species live in Indonesian waters. Marlins, tuna, barracudas, sharks, and manta rays are among the many large fish that swim in the seas around Indonesia. They share the waters with creatures such as dolphins, sea turtles, and whales.

The lakes and rivers of Sulawesi are home to a variety of fish, including beautiful sailfin silversides, halfbeaks, and gobies. The brightly colored Asian arowana inhabits waters flowing throughout thickly wooded swamplands and wetlands, mainly in Borneo.

Plant Life

More than forty thousand species of plants have been identified in the Indonesian islands. Forests cover about 52 percent of Indonesia's land area. About two-thirds of the nation's forests are tropical rain forest in Kalimantan and Papua. These dense, fertile forests grow in areas with abundant rainfall and high humidity. Tropical rain forests feature a thick mix of moss, ferns, climbing vines, and tall trees. The lowlands of eastern Sumatra, southern Kalimantan, and parts of Papua are home to large tracts of mangrove trees. Saltwater kills most trees, but mangroves can grow straight up out of the water. With their looping, fingerlike roots, these trees provide shelter for many fish.

Mangrove trees grow up out of the seafloor. Their tangle of roots provides habitat for many creatures and protects the shoreline by blocking powerful waves.

The World's Largest Flower

Rafflesia arnoldii is one of Indonesia's three national flowers, along with the white jasmine and the moon orchid. Rafflesia is the world's largest and heaviest flower, often reaching 3 feet (1 m) in diameter and weighing up to 24 pounds (11 kg). It does not have leaves, stems, or roots, but instead gathers nutrients and water from the plants it grows on or next to. The flowers of the plant have a reddish-brown color and emit a strong odor that smells like rotting meat. The smell attracts insects such as flies, which pollinate the rare plant. Designated the national "rare flower" in 1993, rafflesia grows mainly in the rain forests and parks of Borneo, Java, and Sumatra.

Tracts of eucalyptus grow in the dry grasslands of the Lesser Sunda Islands. The rainbow eucalyptus features shimmering multicolored bark, which changes color from a bright green to blue, purple, orange, and deep maroon as the tree matures. Trees that thrive at higher altitudes include chestnut, oak, laurel, tea, magnolia, sandalwood, and ebony.

Roughly five thousand varieties of orchids have been identified in Indonesia. Among them are the tiny *Taeniophyllum*, whose flowers grow to only half an inch wide. Also known as the minute orchid, it grows on the underside of branches and lower tree trunks. Exotic plants include the carnivorous pitcher plant, which traps crawling insects and flies in its liquid-filled cupped leaf. The insects drown in the liquid. As their bodies dissolve, they provide the pitcher plant with nutrients it needs to survive.

A logger cuts up logs from an Indonesian forest. Between 2000 and 2012, Indonesia lost 15 million acres (6 million hectares) of old-growth forest, lands that had never been logged before.

Preserving Nature

Kalimantan and Java are the centers of the nation's timber industry. Since the 1970s, the legal and illegal expansion of logging operations has resulted in widespread deforestation, or loss of forests, throughout the archipelago. By 2012, Indonesia was losing more forest than any other nation in the world. That year, 3,250 square miles (8,400 sq km) of Indonesian forest was destroyed. Despite government efforts to slow the rate of deforestation and replant cleared areas, the country's lush forestlands are rapidly disappearing. As the forests disappear, many of Indonesia's unusual animals lose their habitat.

Indonesia has created many national parks and nature reserves to help protect its extraordinary environment. These include Bukit Barisan Selatan National Park on the island of Sumatra. This park is home to Sumatran tigers, elephants, sun bears, rhinoceroses, and many more creatures. Several national parks, including Tanjung Puting, Gunung Palung, and Sebangau, are known for their orangutan populations. Indonesia also has nine national parks that are largely marine environments. These include Cenderawasih Bay National Park in West Papua, the largest marine park in Indonesia. It covers eighteen islands, many miles of coastline, and large expanses of water where whale sharks, sea turtles, and many other creatures swim.

Tanjung Puting National Park

Tanjung Puting National Park in central Borneo is one of Indonesia's greatest natural wonders. The park spreads across 1,600 square miles (4,100 sq km), incorporating a diverse range of habitats, including mangrove swamps, beach forests, and swamp forests. The Dutch colonial government established the park in the 1930s to protect orangutans and proboscis monkeys (left). Other species found in the preserve include clouded leopards, Malaysian sun bears, deer, and wild cattle known as banteng. The park is also home to crocodiles, snakes and lizards, insects, butterflies, and more than 230 varieties of birds. Illegal mining and logging operations have destroyed some of the park's forest and have threatened wildlife in the park. A program of reforestation and animal protection conducted by Indonesia's Friends of the National Parks Foundation, however, has helped to restore much of the park to its former natural state.

CHAPTER 4

Where Kingdoms Once Ruled

IN 1891, A DUTCH DOCTOR NAMED EUGÈNE DUBOIS discovered fossil remains of a humanlike creature on the island of Java. Experts believe the remains, an early species of humans called *Homo erectus*, date from between 700,000 and 500,000 years ago. Dubois's discovery was nicknamed Java Man. These ancient people had an apelike large brow and jutting jaw, and probably used stone tools and lived in caves.

Opposite: **A reconstruction of Java Man. He would have stood about 5 feet 8 inches (1.7 m) tall.**

Early Indonesia

The first modern humans probably arrived in the Indonesian islands about seventy thousand years ago, as people spread out from other parts of Asia. Over the centuries, other waves of migrants arrived. Between 4,500 and 3,500 years ago, people traveled from the island of Taiwan, off the Asian mainland, through the Philippine Islands to Indonesia. They introduced new planting techniques such as wet-rice cultivation, a process of growing rice in flooded fields.

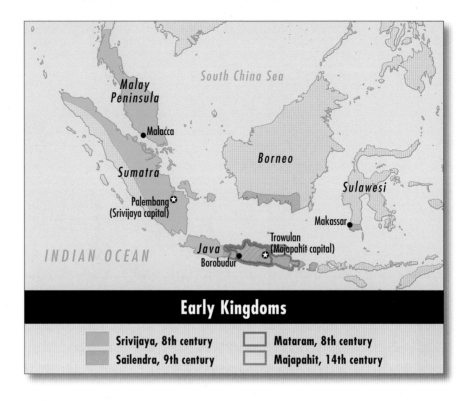

Early Kingdoms

| Srivijaya, 8th century | Mataram, 8th century |
| Sailendra, 9th century | Majapahit, 14th century |

The sea and the winds helped Indonesians reach other parts of the world. By two thousand years ago, people from Borneo had settled on the island of Madagascar, off the east coast of Africa.

The Rise of Kingdoms

In the first century CE, Indian culture and religion began to exert a strong influence on the Indonesian archipelago. Indonesians and Indians exchanged trade goods and ideas. The Indian concept of kingship took root in Indonesia. Indians also introduced Hinduism and Buddhism, two religions that arose in India.

Indonesian coastal communities that had adopted Indian religions began to develop into small, well-organized kingdoms. By the seventh century, an Indian-influenced Buddhist kingdom called Srivijaya had emerged along the coast of eastern Sumatra. The kingdom's lifeblood was the sea. Srivijaya developed successful trade and political relationships with India, Persia (present-day Iran), Arabia (present-day Saudi Arabia), and China, as well as with other places in the Malay Archipelago. Traders came to exchange spices, incense, and textiles for gems and wood, grown in Indonesia's abundant forests. The kingdom became an important center of learning and a Buddhist religious center. Srivijaya dominated the region for about six hundred years. It finally declined by the fourteenth century, eventually splitting into smaller kingdoms.

In the early eighth century, a Hindu kingdom called Mataram developed in Java. At first relying on rice farming, Mataram eventually developed a substantial sea trading network. Mataram declined as the Buddhist Sailendra kingdom rose to power. The Sailendra built Borobudur, a magnificent monumental Buddhist temple in central Java, completed in the year 825.

A large guardian figure sits on the grounds of Prambanan, a Hindu temple built during the Mataram kingdom.

By the fourteenth century a powerful Hindu empire based in Java called Majapahit had become the trading and cultural center of Indonesia. Rice production and trade fueled the empire's economy. Majapahit boasted a sophisticated system of government, fine arts and crafts, and grand palaces and temples.

The Coming of Islam

Traders also brought the new religion of Islam to the archipelago. Islam had emerged on the Arabian Peninsula in the seventh century. Arab traders introduced Indonesia to Islam in Aceh, on the northern tip of Sumatra, in the 700s. By the thirteenth century, most people in Sumatra had accepted the faith. In 1527, the Majapahit empire fell to the new Islamic state of Demak, on Java's north coast.

By this time, leaders from coastal towns and small inland kingdoms throughout Indonesia had converted to Islam. This conversion strengthened these rulers' ties to the port city of Malacca on the Malay Peninsula in mainland Asia because it was a major center of Islam. As the Islamic trade network blossomed, the religion established a stronger foothold throughout the islands. In the sixteenth century, several powerful Muslim kingdoms dominated the archipelago, including the Malacca kingdom in Java and the Makassar kingdom in Sulawesi.

Europeans Arrive

The Portuguese were the first Europeans to arrive in Indonesia. They landed in the islands in the late 1400s, hoping to gain control of the spice trade. The profits made by the Portuguese

on the trade of nutmeg, mace, and cloves attracted other European traders to the islands. In the subsequent struggle for trade domination among Portugal, Spain, England, and the Netherlands, it was the Dutch who won.

The first Dutch expedition to Indonesia arrived in 1596. Four ships landed in Maluku after a fourteen-month journey in which half of the crew members died. The ships returned to the Netherlands with a cargo of valuable spices. Year after year, more Dutch ships came to the region.

The Dutch seized control of the Javanese kingdom of Jayakarta (modern-day Jakarta) and renamed it Batavia in 1619. After numerous bloody battles with Indonesians, they gained control of Banda, Sulawesi, and other spice-producing islands. The Dutch killed thousands of Indonesians and seized enormous tracts of land. By the end of the seventeenth century, the Dutch had complete control of the production of spice, sugar, coffee, pepper, tea, and cotton.

Dutch merchants in Batavia, today's Jakarta, in the 1600s. Throughout the seventeenth century, the Dutch gained control of the trade of spices such as pepper, cloves, and nutmeg.

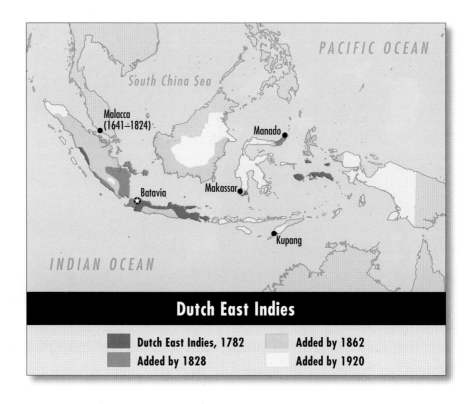

Dutch East Indies

- Dutch East Indies, 1782
- Added by 1828
- Added by 1862
- Added by 1920

To manage their flourishing trade empire, the Dutch established the Dutch East India Company, with headquarters in Batavia. Operating under the control of the Dutch government, this powerful company had the authority to negotiate treaties, wage war, and, of course, engage in trade.

For the next two hundred years, the Dutch tightened their grip on Indonesia, which it called the Dutch East Indies. When the Dutch East India Company took control of Java, they forced the people to grow crops. Angry and frustrated, the Javanese rose up against the Dutch in a series of revolts. The cost of putting down the uprisings was high and drained the financial resources of the company. In 1799, it went bankrupt, and Indonesia officially became a Dutch colony. The newly created colony was called the Dutch East Indies.

In the early 1800s, during the Napoleonic Wars in Europe, the Netherlands lost their Indonesian colony to the British. Life in the islands improved under the brief governorship of Sir Thomas Stamford Raffles. In Java, Raffles initiated several reforms, including improvements in the legal system. He also attempted to abolish the Dutch program of forced labor. In 1816, at the conclusion of the war in Europe, the Dutch regained control of Indonesia.

Diponegoro led Indonesian forces in the Java War. The conflict weakened the Dutch, and Diponegoro remains a national hero today.

The Freedom Movement

The Dutch quickly resumed their colonial policies, exploiting the spice trade and draining the islands of their substantial resources. Meanwhile, most Indonesians were poor, starving, uneducated, and all but enslaved. Fighting often erupted between local populations and Dutch troops.

In 1825, Diponegoro, a Javanese prince, led an uprising against the Dutch, in what is known as the Java War. For five years, Diponegoro rallied wealthy Indonesians and peasants against well-armed Dutch troops. More than two hundred thousand Javanese and eight thousand Dutch died in the conflict, many from disease and starvation. The fighting ended when Diponegoro was arrested.

Indonesian efforts to organize resistance to Dutch rule began to progress in the early twentieth century. In 1908, a group of medical students in Java formed Budi Utomo (noble conduct), Indonesia's first modern political group. In the next twelve years, additional organizations were formed to challenge Dutch colonial rule. Among them was the Indonesian Communist Party, which led several ill-fated rebellions against the Dutch in Sumatra and Java.

In 1927, a former Javanese engineer named Sukarno formed the Indonesian Nationalist Party. A gifted speaker and talented leader, Sukarno roused his fellow Indonesians with the hopeful pledge of unity, "One People, One Language, One Nation." In 1929, Dutch officials arrested Sukarno, and he was later exiled from Java.

Women's Rights Pioneer

Raden Adjeng Kartini was the daughter of a Javanese nobleman working for the Dutch colonial government. Kartini was concerned about the lack of educational opportunities Indonesians, especially the women, were given under Dutch rule. In 1903, she opened the first Indonesian primary school for local girls. Later in her life, she wrote letters to a fellow feminist and Dutch officials in Holland describing the poor treatment of Indonesians. The letters were published in the book *Out of Dark Comes Light*. Kartini's writings attracted attention in the Netherlands and helped change the way the Dutch viewed women in Indonesia. Her letters also encouraged other Indonesians in the fight for independence.

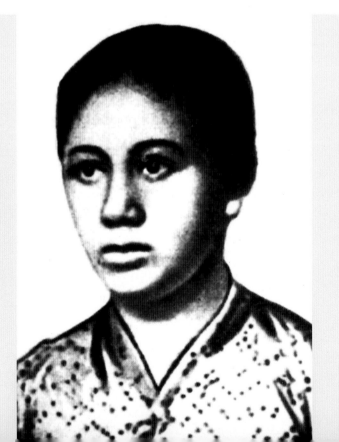

Under Japanese Control

When Japan invaded the archipelago during World War II (1939–1945), the Dutch finally met their match. The Japanese quickly took control, arrested all Europeans, and established their own system of government. At first, the Indonesians welcomed the newcomers. They believed the invaders would liberate them from the Dutch. The Japanese, however, treated the Indonesians even more cruelly than the islanders' former colonial masters had. They enslaved the Indonesians, forcing them to produce food and supplies for Japanese troops.

On August 15, 1945, Japan surrendered, ending the war—and their control in Indonesia. Two days later, Sukarno—who had been freed by the Japanese in 1942—declared Indonesia's independence. On August 18, a new constitution was announced, and Sukarno assumed the presidency. The nation of Indonesia was born.

Japanese troops come ashore in Borneo during World War II. Japan occupied Indonesia for three years during the war.

The Final Victory

British troops went to Indonesia to deal with the Japanese and free Europeans from Japanese prisons. During this period of uncertainty, the Dutch once again tried to reassert control. They claimed Sukarno was a supporter of the Japanese. Meanwhile, Sukarno tried to establish his new government. Tensions increased, and fighting erupted between the Indonesian army and the British troops. In October 1945, a violent battle in Surabaya resulted in thousands of British and Indonesian casualties.

The British bombed Indonesian positions in Surabaya and allowed Dutch troops to land in Java. Dutch and British forces joined together to fight the growing armed resistance of the Indonesian people. When the Dutch launched major attacks against the Indonesians in 1947 and 1948, however, they were sharply criticized by world leaders.

Finally, in January 1949, the United Nations demanded that the Dutch recognize the Indonesian government. On December 27, 1949, the Dutch gave up their claim to Indonesia. Sukarno became the first president of the new Republic of Indonesia.

The Path to Democracy

Despite its newfound independence, Indonesia faced uncertainty and instability. Dozens of political parties fought for leadership. Indonesians were widely divided along religious, political, and ethnic lines. The economy was in shambles, with inflation running high. Corruption and inefficiency were widespread in the government. Sukarno responded by

Indonesia's First President

Sukarno (1901–1970) was born in Surabaya, the only son of a poor Javanese schoolteacher and his Balinese wife. As a student, Sukarno mastered many languages, including several Indonesian languages, Arabic, Dutch, German, English, and French. Later on, he also learned Japanese. In high school, he developed friendships with some of Indonesia's most prominent nationalist leaders and began to think and write about independence from the Dutch.

In 1928, he cofounded the Indonesian Nationalist Party. Sukarno's goal was to unite the divergent peoples of the Indonesian islands into a single, independent nation. He was arrested in 1929 by the Dutch colonial secret police for disturbing the peace. During his trial the following year, he made a series of speeches against Dutch colonialism that gained him widespread support.

Sukarno returned to Jakarta in 1942 after years of forced exile by Dutch authorities. During the early 1940s, he worked with the Japanese during their occupation of Indonesia in the hopes of keeping the Dutch out of the East Indies. Through radio broadcasts, he became well known among Indonesians as a strong leader.

On August 17, 1945, Sukarno announced Indonesia's independence. The new nation's stability, however, was in doubt. For years, Indonesians fought the Dutch and the British and then each other for control of the country. Thousands of people were imprisoned or killed. Discontent, demonstrations, and riots continued throughout much of Sukarno's presidency.

By 1966, Sukarno had lost his popular support. On April 11, he signed a presidential order that turned over the presidency to General Suharto, who had recently seized command of the Indonesian army. The disgraced former president was placed under house arrest in March 1967 and died three years later at age sixty-nine.

Ethnic tensions frequently flared in Indonesia's early years. In 1963, violent demonstrations against British and Malaysians shook Jakarta.

creating a "guided democracy," which actually increased his authority and made him, in effect, a dictator. In 1960, he eliminated the parliament House of Representatives, replacing it with his own new People's Representative Council. In 1963, he declared himself Indonesia's Ruler for Life.

At home, Indonesians grew restless and alarmed at Sukarno's policies. Most people continued to live in poverty, without education and health care, while he lived in luxury. Abroad, the United States and other countries were distrustful of Sukarno's ties to the Soviet Union and China, two powerful communist nations.

In September 1965, the military, with the support of the communist party, attempted a coup, or overthrow, of Sukarno's government. The coup failed, but it set off violent protests against Sukarno. In retaliation for the coup attempt, Sukarno's supporters killed at least three hundred thousand communists and suspected communists. Another 1.5 million people were imprisoned. With this mass slaughter, Sukarno destroyed the Communist Party of Indonesia, but he also upset the balance of power in the government. He was forced to resign in 1967 and was replaced by Indonesian army general Suharto.

A "New Order"

Suharto promised reform under a program called the New Order. In practice, however, he continued Sukarno's authoritarian ways. Suharto eliminated opposition political parties. He used the military to keep an eye on the activities of government officials and civilians. Uprisings demanding greater

Indonesian soldiers guard a group of suspected communists. Hundreds of thousands of people were slaughtered during Indonesia's anticommunist frenzy of 1965 to 1966.

political freedoms were quickly put down and their leaders were imprisoned. Government corruption ran wild.

Indonesia's economy, however, improved under Suharto. International demand for Indonesia's oil brought in much-needed revenue. By restoring relations with the United States and other Western nations that Sukarno had alienated, foreign aid and investment flowed into Indonesia. The government improved transportation, education, and health care.

Then, in 1997, a financial crisis swept through Asia. Banks collapsed, and millions of people lost their jobs. Roughly half the population was in poverty, without money to buy food. In

President Suharto (in black) meets officials in Myanmar (formerly Burma) in 1997. The Indonesian economy grew during his three decades in office, but many Indonesians resented his authoritarian rule.

Indonesian students hold a demonstration in Jakarta in 1999 demanding free elections. Student protests had helped force Suharto from office the year before.

1998, three days of rioting erupted. More than two thousand buildings in Jakarta were damaged or destroyed, and 1,200 people died.

Many people blamed Suharto for the country's troubles. Students took to the streets demanding his resignation. Suharto lost support in the government and military, and on May 21, 1998, he resigned. Vice President B. J. Habibie was installed as president. He was replaced in the 1999 election by Muslim leader Abdurrahman Wahid.

Independence for Timor-Leste

When Indonesia proclaimed its independence in 1945, the island of Timor belonged to two nations. The western half belonged to Indonesia, while the eastern half belonged to Portugal. In 1974, a military coup in Portugal replaced Portugal's dictatorship with a democracy. The new Portuguese government chose to withdraw from Timor and its other colonies. In December 1975, the Indonesian military invaded East Timor and claimed the entire island. Throughout the 1970s and 1980s, Indonesian troops battled the East Timorese (right). More than two hundred thousand people died from battle, starvation, or disease.

In 1999, Indonesian president B. J. Habibie agreed to allow the people of East Timor to decide for themselves whether they wanted independence. Almost 80 percent of East Timorese voted for independence. Furious, Indonesian troops and local militia groups with ties to the military went on a rampage. Buildings were burned, and homes and businesses were destroyed. Tens of thousands of civilians fled in terror. United Nations troops were sent in to quell the violence and maintain order. In May 2002, East Timor declared its independence, becoming the nation of Timor-Leste (left).

More Recent Times

Wahid angered conservative Muslims because of his support for religious tolerance. Military leaders were angered by his plan to hold them responsible for the violence the armed forces waged against separatists in East Timor during the 1970s and 1980s. In 2001, the Indonesian legislature voted Wahid out of office. His vice president, Megawati Sukarnoputri, Sukarno's daughter, became ruler.

During her time in office, Sukarnoputri had to cope with acts of terrorism by extremist Muslims striking targets frequented by Westerners. In 2002, a radical Islamic group bombed a Bali nightclub, killing more than 200 people and injuring roughly 250 more. This attack and others that followed damaged Indonesia's tourism industry.

Into the Future

In recent years, the Indonesian economy has been growing rapidly. Poverty has been drastically reduced since the late 1990s, and today only roughly 12 percent of Indonesia's population lives below the poverty line. In 2013, the country's economy was growing at an annual rate of 5.3 percent, whereas the growth rate of the U.S. economy was only 1.6 percent.

Democracy has also been growing stronger in Indonesia. In October 2004, Indonesia held a direct presidential election, the first since 1955. Retired army general Susilo Bambang Yudhoyono defeated Sukarnoputri. His government performed well in the aftermath of the devastating December 2004 tsunami. In 2005, the government also negotiated a cease-fire agreement with separatists in Aceh, in northern Sumatra, who had been fighting Indonesian forces for more than a decade. Then, in 2014, Indonesians elected Joko Widodo president. He is the first Indonesian president to come from a poor background.

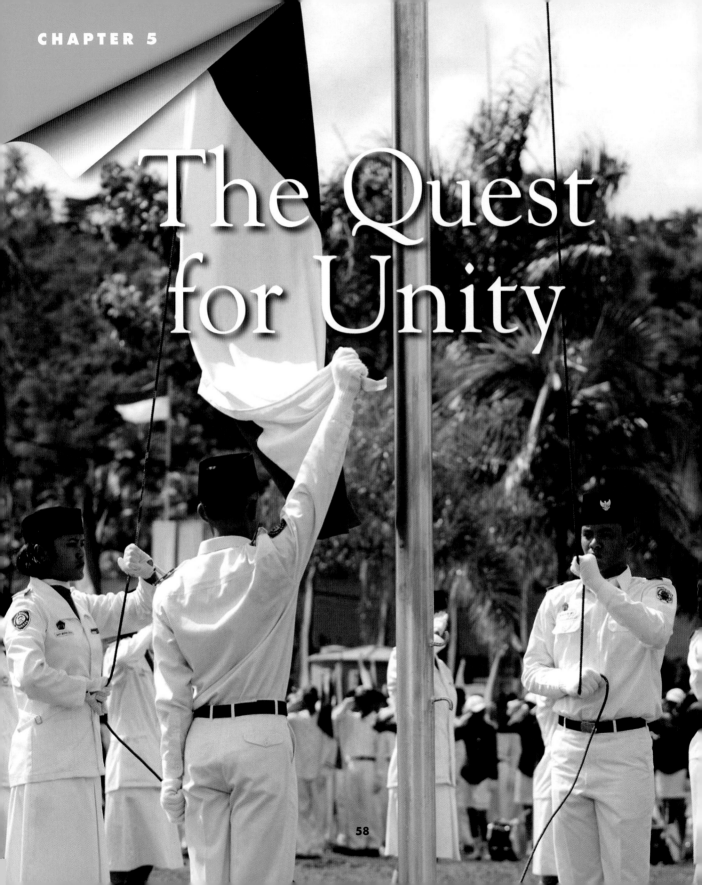

CHAPTER 5

The Quest for Unity

I N 1945, SUKARNO MADE A SPEECH IN WHICH HE outlined a philosophy called Pancasila (Five Principles) to guide the new nation. The first principle was belief in one God. This principle stated that Indonesians had freedom of religion as long as they believed in a single god. The second principle was humanity and justice, which called for respect for the lives of others. Third was nationalism, which encouraged Indonesians to live as one and work for the benefit of the entire nation, rather than particular ethnic groups. Fourth was Indonesian-style government, which called for political decisions to be made through fair negotiations and compromise. The final principle was social justice, which stated that the nation's natural resources should be used to meet the basic needs of the people.

Opposite: **Young people raise the Indonesian flag on a holiday honoring the nation's independence.**

The National Emblem

The national emblem, or coat of arms, of Indonesia is called the Garuda Pancasila. The Garuda—an ancient mythical bird—symbolizes energy, nature, and the greatness of the country. The eight feathers on the bird's tail, seventeen feathers on each wing, and forty-five on its neck represent the date of Indonesia's independence, August 17, 1945. The symbols on the shield stand for Pancasila, the five values that make up Indonesia's national philosophy. The Garuda grips a white ribbon inscribed with the national motto, *"Bhinneka Tunggal Ika"* ("Unity in Diversity"). President Sukarno supervised the design of the coat of arms, which was officially adopted as the national emblem on February 11, 1950.

The Pancasila was incorporated into the nation's constitution to unite all Indonesians, who for centuries had been separated from one another by geographic distance and differing languages and religions.

The Structure of Government

Indonesia is a republic with three branches of government: executive, legislative, and judicial. The executive branch is composed of the president and vice president. The people directly elect the president and vice president to five-year terms. Both the president and vice president are limited to two terms. The president may develop regulations to carry out the laws approved by the legislative branch. He or she is also the supreme commander of the armed forces, and can

The national flag of Indonesia is called the *Sang Saka Merah Putih*, which means "The Sacred Red and White." It is based on the nine-striped red-and-white banner of the 13th-century Majapahit Empire in East Java. The flag was introduced at the Indonesian Independence Day festivities on August 17, 1945, and officially adopted one month later. It features two horizontal bands of equal size, red on the top and white on the bottom. The red represents gallantry and freedom, and the white symbolizes justice and purity.

declare war or negotiate peace in agreement with the People's Representative Council. The president appoints cabinet members, who oversee a number of areas. Among them are the ministers of agriculture, transportation, defense, energy, health, finance, foreign affairs, and tourism.

President of the People

In 2014, Indonesians elected Joko Widodo president. Widodo is the first leader of Indonesia who is not from a military or elite background. He grew up in a slum, and as a young child had to work to earn money for school supplies. At age twelve, he began helping at his father's furniture workshop, but he never quit school. After attending university, Widodo went into business before turning to politics. At the time of the presidential election, he was serving as governor of the Jakarta Capital Region. As governor, he improved flood control, provided health care for all, and began programs to reduce government corruption.

National Government of Indonesia

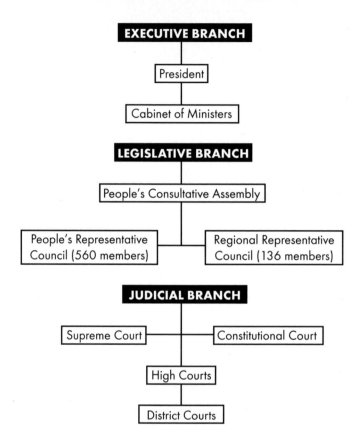

EXECUTIVE BRANCH

President

Cabinet of Ministers

LEGISLATIVE BRANCH

People's Consultative Assembly

People's Representative Council (560 members)

Regional Representative Council (136 members)

JUDICIAL BRANCH

Supreme Court

Constitutional Court

High Courts

District Courts

The legislative branch is known as the People's Consultative Assembly (MPR). It is made up of two bodies: the People's Representative Council (DPR) and the Regional Representative Council (DPD). The DPR is the main legislative body in the Indonesian government. In 2014, the DPR had 560 members, who are elected for five-year terms. The DPR drafts and votes on laws, and creates the annual budget with the president.

The less-powerful DPD represents regional interests in the national government. In 2014, the DPD included 136 members. The DPD can propose bills to the DPR regarding regional issues, such as the use of natural resources and finances, and the merging of regions. It is required to provide its opinion on the national budget and on bills affecting taxes, education, and religion.

The judicial branch includes the Supreme Court, the Constitutional Court, and lower courts. The Supreme Court is the nation's highest court and final court of appeals. It is respon-

The People's Consultative Assembly meets in a large building in South Jakarta.

The National Anthem

Wage Rudolf Supratman composed "Indonesia Raya" ("Great Indonesia") in 1928 as a call to all Indonesians to support ethnic and cultural unity in their homeland. The song was sung at political rallies and printed in newspapers in a gesture of defiance against Dutch authorities. The first stanza of the song was chosen as Indonesia's national anthem when the country declared its independence in 1945.

Indonesian lyrics

Indonesia tanah airku
Tanah tumpah darahku
Di sanalah aku berdiri
Jadi pandu ibuku.

Indonesia kebangsaanku
Bangsa dan tanah airku
Marilah kita berseru
"Indonesia bersatu!"

Hiduplah tanahku, hiduplah negeriku
Bangsaku, rakyatku, semuanya
Bangunlah jiwanya, bangunlah badannya
Untuk Indonesia Raya.

Indonesia Raya, merdeka, merdeka!
Tanahku, negeriku yang kucinta
Indonesia Raya, merdeka, merdeka!
Hiduplah Indonesia Raya!

English translation

Indonesia, my homeland
The land where I shed my blood
Right there, I stand
To be a guide of my motherland.

Indonesia, my nationality
My nation and my homeland
Let us exclaim
"Indonesia unites!"

Long live my land, long live my country
My nation, my people, entirely
Let us build its soul, let us build its body
For the Great Indonesia.

Great Indonesia, independent and free!
My land, my country that I love
Great Indonesia, independent and free!
Long live Great Indonesia!

sible for reexamining cases if new evidence in them emerges. The Supreme Court also oversees lower courts. These include high courts, which hear appeals from district courts.

The Constitutional Court was established in 2003 as part of the government's effort to reform the judicial process. It reviews the constitutionality of laws, resolves disputes among different branches of government, and decides disputes over election results.

Hamdan Zoelva became the chief justice of the Constitutional Court in 2013. Eight other justices also serve on the court.

Political Parties

Many political parties vie for power in Indonesia. In 2014, representatives from ten political parties were elected to the People's Representative Council. The Indonesian Democratic Party of Struggle, running on the Indonesian national philosophy, Pancasila, won 109 seats, the most of any party. Four

Supporters of the Indonesian Democratic Party of Struggle attend a rally. The party's symbol is a bull.

moderate Islamic parties combined to win 175 seats, or 31 percent of the total number of seats.

Regional Government

Indonesia is divided into thirty-four provinces and special regions. Each is led by a governor. The five special regions are Aceh, Yogyakarta, Papua, West Papua, and Jakarta Special Capital Region. The provinces are subdivided into districts called *kecamatan*.

A Look at the Capital City

Jakarta, Indonesia's capital and largest city, is home to roughly 10,188,000 people. Located on the northwest coast of Java, the city traces its history to the fourth century, as part of one of the oldest Hindu kingdoms in Indonesia. By the thirteenth century, the city, then called Sunda Kelapa, had developed into a small port that was part of a large, thriving Hindu kingdom. By the 1500s, it was a major seaport and center of trade. The city was renamed Jayakarta (Glorious Victory) by its Muslim conquerors in about 1530.

In 1618, the Dutch destroyed most of the city during battles against Indonesian forces, and renamed the city Batavia. The city served as the economic center of the Dutch colonial empire for the next 300 years. The city was renamed Jakarta during the Japanese occupation of the 1940s.

Today, the city is a center for industries such as electronics, chemicals, communications, and finance.

Tourism is also important. Most of Jakarta's visitors come from other parts of Indonesia. Favorite tourist attractions include Ragunan Zoo, the old port of Sunda Kelapa, and Ancol Dreamland, a theme park along Jakarta's waterfront.

Major landmarks in Jakarta include the National Monument (above), a 433-foot (132 m) tower that commemorates the fight for Indonesian independence. The nearby Istiqlal Mosque is the largest mosque in Southeast Asia. Standing in front of the mosque is the Jakarta Cathedral, a Roman Catholic house of worship built in 1901. The Jakarta History Museum, located in the Old Town section of Jakarta was once the city hall of Batavia. Today, the museum features artifacts displaying the early history of Jakarta and its surrounding regions. Another popular attraction is Taman Mini Indonesia Indah, a park that features cultural exhibits from across Indonesia.

Other areas of the city feature modern homes, shopping malls, hotels, skyscrapers, and sports arenas. At 860 feet (262 m) tall, the sleek Wisma 46 is Indonesia's tallest building. Gelora Bung Karno Stadium is used for soccer matches and seats more than 88,000 spectators. The stadium also hosts political rallies, rock concerts, and religious gatherings.

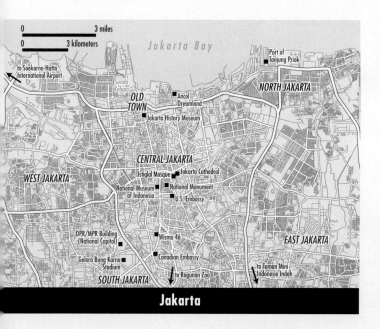

Jakarta

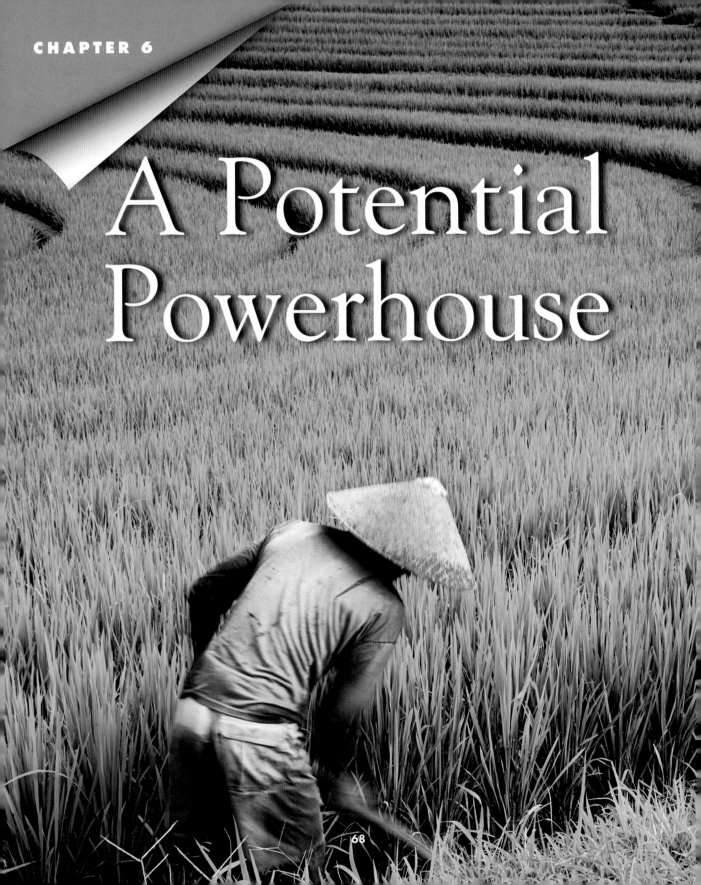

CHAPTER 6

A Potential Powerhouse

NDONESIA'S ECONOMIC FUTURE LOOKS BRIGHT. THE country is blessed with an abundance of natural resources, including oil, natural gas, minerals, and rubber. It has a huge labor force of 120 million people. And, today, Indonesia boasts the largest economy in Southeast Asia. Many experts believe it is poised to become an international economic powerhouse.

Opposite: **A farmer tends a rice field on Bali.**

Agriculture, Fishing, and Forestry

About 40 percent of the Indonesian labor force works in agriculture, a decline of nearly 10 percent in the last three decades. Roughly 8 percent of Indonesia's land is used for agriculture. Most commercial crops are grown on large farms called estates. Many Indonesians also farm their own small plots or personal gardens.

Rice is the most widely grown crop. The nation ranks third in the world in rice production, behind China and India. Indonesia's rice is grown in two different ways. On the outer islands, where the soil is not particularly rich, rice is grown

Indonesia's official unit of currency is the rupiah (IDR). Coins come in denominations of 50, 100, 200, 500, and 1,000 rupiahs. Indonesian bills, or banknotes, are issued with values of 1,000; 2,000; 5,000; 10,000; 20,000; 50,000; and 100,000 rupiahs.

The banknotes feature colorful depictions of Indonesian history, architecture, and culture. The 1,000-rupiah note shows Pattimura, a nineteenth-century soldier who fought for independence from the Dutch, and a picture of fishermen on a boat sailing past islands. The 2,000-rupiah note depicts Antasari, a pro-independence sultan from Banjar, and Indonesian women performing the *dayak*, a traditional dance of Borneo. In 2014, 12,200 rupiahs equaled US$1.

using a technique called slash and burn. To clear new land for farming, people cut trees and other vegetation and then burn the remaining plants on the land. New crops can be planted in the burned land for only two or three years using this technique. After that, the soil must not be farmed until it replenishes its store of nutrients. Widespread slash-and-burn farming also contributes to air pollution. On Indonesia's inner islands, which have abundant fertile soils, farmers grow rice on terraced hillsides, or in wet rice fields. The soil is not stripped of its nutrients, allowing it to produce several crops each year.

Indonesian farmers also grow a wide range of other crops. Indonesia is the world's largest producer of palm oil, accounting for more than half of world output. Palm oil is grown mainly on large estates in Kalimantan and Sumatra. Other important crops include cassava (a root), corn, soybeans, and sweet potatoes. Medan is home to large plantations that produce tobacco, rubber, tea, cloves, and coffee.

Small-scale farmers own almost all of the livestock in Indonesia. Cattle, goats, sheep, chickens, pigs, horses, and ducks are raised in the tens of millions. Beef, pork, poultry, and eggs are some of the country's most important food crops.

Fish is an important source of protein in the Indonesian diet. More than three million households are involved in the fishing industry. Indonesian fishers export large quantities of shrimp and tuna, mainly to Japan.

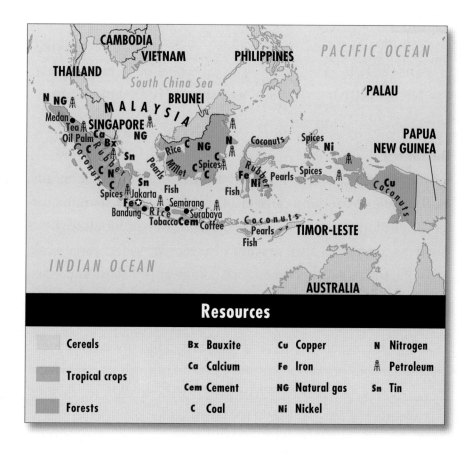

Resources

Cereals	**Bx** Bauxite	**Cu** Copper	**N** Nitrogen
	Ca Calcium	**Fe** Iron	**Ӎ** Petroleum
Tropical crops	**Cem** Cement	**NG** Natural gas	**Sn** Tin
Forests	**C** Coal	**Ni** Nickel	

What Indonesia, Grows, Makes, and Mines

AGRICULTURE (2011)

Rice	65,740,946 metric tons
Cassava	24,009,624 metric tons
Oil palm fruit	21,449,000 metric tons

MANUFACTURING (2009, VALUE ADDED)

Chemicals	US$12,655,000,000
Food	US$12,364,000,000
Transportation equipment	US$10,175,000,000

MINING

Oil (2013)	939,710 barrels per day
Tin (2010)	43,258 metric tons
Nickel (2010)	210,000 metric tons

Industry

Manufacturing is the largest part of Indonesia's economy, accounting for about a quarter of it. Many of the manufacturers in Indonesia are small-scale businesses producing goods such as furniture and textiles. In recent years, large-scale manufacturing has become more common in Indonesia. Cars, chemicals, and electronics equipment are all important products manufactured in Indonesia.

Oil and natural gas have become major money earners, particularly in Sumatra. Indonesia is the number one producer of petroleum in Southeast Asia and has the world's tenth-largest reserves of natural gas. The Indonesian government owns all oil and natural gas rights in the country but maintains agreements with foreign firms to drill for the oil and refine it. Chevron Pacific Indonesia, a company based in the United States, is the largest oil producer in Indonesia, accounting for roughly 40 percent of the country's total output. Pertamina, a state-owned corporation, is Indonesia's second-leading producer of crude oil. About two-thirds of Indonesia's petroleum is exported. Much of the nation's natural gas is sold to Japan.

Indonesia also has large reserves of other valuable minerals. The country is the world's second-leading producer of tin,

Indonesia uses both modern and traditional methods of oil mining. In the Wonocolo forest in East Java, workers collect oil in traditional ways.

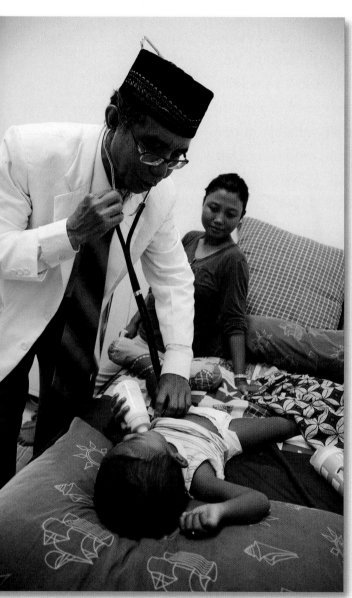

A doctor examines a baby in Aceh. Medical workers are part of the service sector of the economy.

behind China. Tin mining occurs primarily on the islands of Bangka and Belitung in the Java Sea. In the 1980s, Indonesia became one of the world's leading producers of nickel. Today, it ranks second only to the Philippines in annual production. Nickel is mined mainly in Sulawesi. Large quantities of copper and gold are mined in the Ertsberg and Grasberg Mountains in Papua. Bauxite, used in the production of aluminum, is found on Bintan Island, off the southern tip of the Malay Peninsula.

Service Industries

Service industries—businesses that provide services rather than products—employ 48 percent of Indonesia's workforce. These industries include tourism, transportation, sales, communication, finance, and government jobs. Indonesia's natural beauty—shimmering oceans, pristine beaches, towering volcanoes, and magnificent climate—attracts tourists from around the world. In 2013, nearly nine million visitors entered Indonesia. The most popular tourist destinations are Bali, Java, and Sumatra. From lush rain forests to deep-sea diving sites to surfing locations to countless cultural attractions, Indonesia has lots to offer travelers the world over.

Getting Around

Historically, Indonesia's vast ocean distances and rugged island terrain have made transportation and communication between its people highly challenging. Beginning in the 1970s, major efforts were undertaken to upgrade the country's roads, railroads, ports, and airports.

Traveling by road is the most important form of transportation in Indonesia. The country has about 300,000 miles (500,000 km) of roadways, of which 56 percent are paved. Local governments encourage the growth of bus services to reduce the number of motor vehicles using the nation's highways and urban streets. Bus service is readily available in major cities. Minibuses or minivans provide transportation in rural areas and between smaller towns. Personal car usage is on the rise throughout Indonesia, as car sales increase dramatically each year. More than twice the number of cars was sold in 2014 as in 2008, an increase from roughly 600,000 to more than 1.3 million. Traffic jams are common in major cities throughout the archipelago.

Of the nation's 3,100 miles (5,000 km) of railroad track, roughly 75 percent is located in Java. Most trains are used for passenger transportation, although railroads are becoming increasingly more important for hauling industrial goods such as cement, coal, and freight.

A worker unloads lumber from a *pinisi*, a type of ship that is often used to transport cargo between islands.

Transportation between the islands is provided by a variety of ferries and other ships. Traditional two-mast wooden ships called *pinisi* are still widely used to carry freight. Car ferries run twenty-four-hour service on the busy crossings between Sumatra, Java, and Bali. Other ferries travel between Sumatra and the nation of Malaysia. The national shipping company Pelni provides passenger service throughout the archipelago. Major ports and harbors include Tanjung Priok in Jakarta; Belawan in Medan, Sumatra; and Makassar in Sulawesi.

In the early twenty-first century, many new budget airlines began offering service linking all parts of the archipelago. As a result, passenger air transportation throughout Indonesia boomed. Jakarta's Soekarno–Hatta International Airport is the country's main air transportation hub. Other international airports include Husein Sastranegara and Juanda in Java; Kuala Namu in Medan, Sumatra; and Ngurah Rai in Bali.

Communications

Improved telephone communications have made keeping in touch throughout Indonesia easier than ever. The country ranks fourth worldwide in the number of cell phones, with 282 million. That's more phones than there are people in the country.

There are about a dozen nationwide TV stations in Indonesia. But TVRI, a state-owned television station, is the only free channel that people living in remote areas can receive. Many people, however, get cable or satellite TV.

Most newspapers are written in the Indonesian language. The largest and most influential national paper is *Kompas*, with a daily readership of about 1.2 million people. More than two-dozen regional newspapers are also published. English-language newspapers include the *Jakarta Globe*, the *Jakarta Post*, and the *Bali Times*. Chinese- and Japanese-language newspapers can also be found.

As in the rest of the world, Internet usage in Indonesia has skyrocketed recently. In 2000, there were only eight million Internet users in Indonesia. By 2013, more than seventy-one million Indonesians were online.

Most people in Indonesia have cell phones.

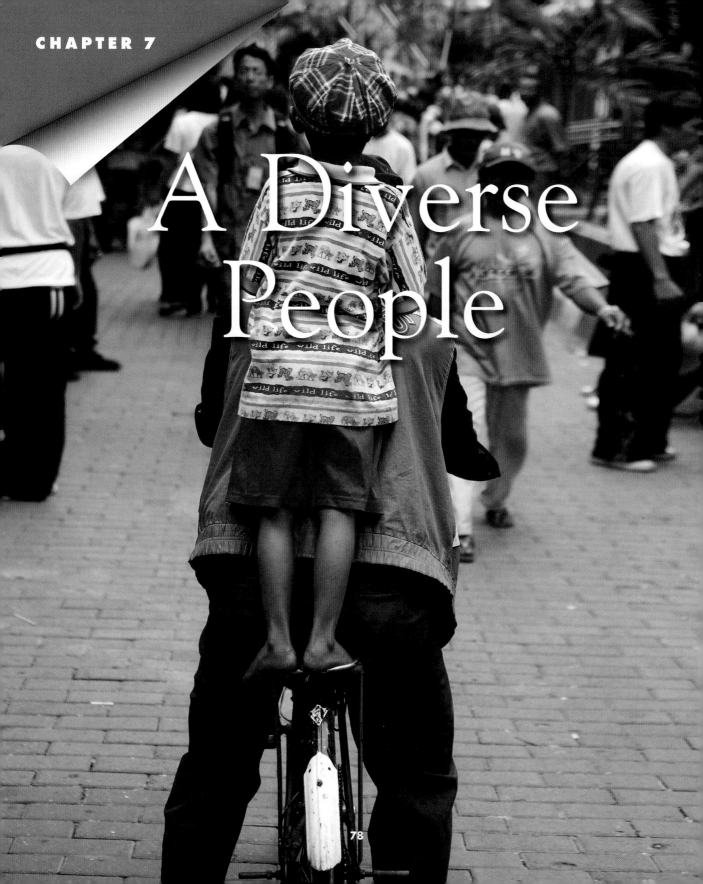

CHAPTER 7

A Diverse People

THE PEOPLE OF INDONESIA ARE DIVERSE NOT JUST from island to island, separated by ocean expanses, but also within each island, separated by towering mountain ranges, rivers, and dense forests. More than three hundred different ethnic groups who speak hundreds of different languages inhabit the various areas of these islands. Despite the distances and vast differences, Indonesians have found a way to remain united.

On Java

The largest of Indonesia's ethnic groups is the Javanese, who make up about 40 percent of the population. They live mainly in Central, Eastern, and Western Java. Ancestors of modern-day Javanese first arrived in the region from Taiwan 4,500 to 3,500 years ago. Throughout Indonesian history, Javanese have traditionally held the most important positions in the government and military. But most Javanese are farmers or factory workers. They usually live in small villages of two hundred or three hundred people.

Sundanese men carry freshly harvested rice during the Seren Taun festival, which celebrates and gives thanks for the bountiful harvest. The festival is held in many different Sundanese villages.

Preserving a Way of Life

The Badui people live in central Java. Ethnically, the Badui belong to the Sundanese group, and speak a form of Sundanese. The Badui number only five thousand to eight thousand people. To preserve their culture from outside influences, the Badui have divided their society into two groups. The inner Badui are the holy members of the community, who live in three sacred villages called Tanah Larangan, or "Forbidden Territory." The holy members, who the Badui believe are descended from gods, do not allow any type of technology into their villages and discourage outsiders from visiting. The outer Badui live in about two-dozen villages on the outskirts of the Forbidden Territory. They have slightly more contact with the outside world. The Badui are forbidden to use any form of transportation or to learn how to write. Doing so, they believe would conflict with the will of gods and spirits.

The Sundanese people, Indonesia's second-largest ethnic group, live mainly in Western Java, Jakarta, and the western part of Central Java. Like the Javanese, the main profession of Sundanese people is farming. Many Sundanese sell food and drink at food stalls or own small businesses that offer clothing and household items.

The Madurese traditionally lived on the island of Madura off the northeastern coast of Java. Over the years, many migrated and settled near the city of Surabaya on the northeastern coast of East Java as well as in western and southern Kalimantan. Most are devoted Muslims. Village life focuses around an Islamic religious center, where a separate religious group is in

An Acehnese man parks his boat in Banda Aceh. Traditional Acehnese boats are usually painted bright colors.

Ethnicity in Indonesia (2010 est.)*	
Javanese	40.1%
Sundanese	15.5%
Malay	3.7%
Batak	3.6%
Madurese	3.0%
Betawi	2.9%
Minangkabau	2.7%
Buginese	2.7%
Bantanese	2.0%
Banjarese	1.7%
Balinese	1.7%
Acehnese	1.4%
Sasak	1.3%
Chinese	1.2%
Other	16.4%

*Total does not equal 100% because of rounding.

charge of worship. On Madura, the Madurese make their living by raising cattle and cultivating rice.

On Sumatra

The Acehnese live at the northernmost tip of Sumatra, with their villages often located in the middle of large rice fields. Traditionally, the Acehnese people have been farmers and craftspeople specializing in metalworking, boatbuilding, and weaving. Northern Sumatra was the first place where Islam arrived in Indonesia, and, today, the Acehnese are considered the most conservative Muslim group in the country.

Other ethnic groups living on Sumatra include the Batak, the Minangkabau, and the Malays. The Batak live in north-central Sumatra. There are six distinct Batak groups in Sumatra, organized into clans, or large family groups. Many Bataks are accomplished musicians and have become singers and bandleaders. Sumatra's central highlands are home to the Minangkabau. Women are highly revered in this society. Clan membership is passed down from a mother to her children, and all property, wealth, and family surnames are passed down from mother to daughter. Men are responsible for the family's religious and political affairs.

The Malays live in Eastern Sumatra. Early Malays were heavily influenced by Hindu Indian voyagers who sailed there from across the Bay of Bengal more than two thousand years ago. Today, most Malays are Muslims who also practice traditional religious beliefs. Traditional Malay houses are built on wooden pilings that raise the houses as high as 8 feet (2.4 m) off the ground. The roofs are usually made of thatch. Homes of wealthier people have wooden plank floors and tile roofs. Other notable ethnic groups on Sumatra include the Lampung and Kubu.

A Minangkabau woman weaves outside of a traditional colorful Minangkabau house.

On Other Islands

The Balinese of Bali and nearby Lombok are primarily Hindu. They devote long hours to preparing temples for religious rituals and ceremonies. The Balinese are known for their arts and crafts. Distinct villages are often dedicated to a particular type of craft, such as painting or woodworking.

Many Balinese men wear a head cloth called an *udeng*.

Sulawesi is home to the Minahasa, Toraja, and Buginese. The Minahasa of northern Sulawesi are primarily Christian, and are mostly of European and Asian descent. The Toraja live in rugged, mountainous regions of central Sulawesi. Most are Christian and still observe traditional forms of ritual practice.

The Dayak include many different ethnic groups that live along rivers in the forests of Kalimantan. Dozens of families live together in communal longhouses hundreds of feet long. Dayaks hunt and fish using blowpipes and spears. Many Dayaks practice Christianity. They also engage in rituals to help them maintain strong relationships with ancestral spirits. Body decoration, such as tattooing, is an important element of Dayak culture. In order to appear more beautiful, many

Into the Afterlife

The death rituals of the Toraja people of South Sulawesi are elaborate. A funeral is often held months or even years after a person dies. This delay allows the family of the deceased to raise enough money for funeral expenses and allows the body time to decay. Once there is nothing left but bones, the Toraja people believe, the soul can be free from the body.

At the death ceremony, the body is placed in a high wooden tower, overlooking the celebration (right). The event features music, sports, singing, ritual dancing, and poetry reading. The richer and more powerful the deceased person was, the costlier and more elaborate

the funeral. Death ceremonies of a wealthy nobleman can last several days and be attended by thousands of people.

Water buffalo are killed during the ritual. Their bodies are arranged on a field where they wait for the spirit of the deceased. The Toraja believe that the dead person rides the souls of the buffalo to reach the afterlife. The higher the rank of the deceased, the more buffalo that are killed. The buffalo's spirits are believed to travel to the afterlife with the deceased, so the person maintains rank in the afterlife. Some of the bodies of the buffalo are given to guests as gifts, providing meat for the community.

On the day of burial, the coffin containing the deceased is placed in a cave high on a cliff. A carved wooden effigy of the dead person is put in the cave overlooking the land (left). Each August, the skeletons of the dead are removed, washed, and dressed in new clothes.

Dayaks wear several heavy metal earrings that stretch their earlobes to shoulder length.

In the easternmost reaches of the archipelago, the Papuans have more in common with their island neighbors in Papua New Guinea than with other Indonesian ethnic groups.

In the past, when Dayak people were young, they would begin wearing heavy brass earrings to stretch their earlobes. Stretched earlobes were considered a sign of beauty and status. Today, the practice is dying out.

Their language, religion, and social customs are similar to native peoples of Australia and those on islands farther east. The Asmat people, in southwestern Papua, had little contact with outsiders until the middle of the twentieth century. Traditionally, they have relied on the bounty of the forest and sea for food. They make flour from a starch they remove from the trunk of the sago palm. They also hunt and fish. For the Dani people, who live farther inland, sweet potatoes and pigs are important foods.

Chinese Indonesians

Roughly 1.2 percent of Indonesia's population is Chinese, descended from Chinese traders who came to the islands hundreds of years ago. During Dutch rule in the late nineteenth century, many Chinese came to Indonesia to work on plantations and in mines. Denied by the Dutch the right to own land, they started businesses. Some became very wealthy, causing resentment among the Indonesians.

Many Chinese were supporters of the Indonesian Communist Party during the 1950s and 1960s, further fueling anger toward them. The hostility boiled over into killings and burnings of Chinese homes and businesses. During his reign, Suharto imposed government restrictions that banned Chinese media and culture in Indonesia. Many Chinese fled

The Asmat people of Papua are renowned for their wood-carving skill. The carved figures typically represent ancestors.

Chinese Indonesians celebrate Chinese New Year at a temple in Jakarta. About half of all Chinese Indonesians live on the island of Java.

the islands. Today, Chinese have the same rights as other ethnic groups. They can practice their culture and use the Chinese language, as well as establish Chinese schools.

From Country to City

With an estimated population of 253,609,643 people, Indonesia is the fourth most populous nation in the world. Only China, India, and the United States have larger populations. About 57 percent of Indonesians live on Java. Slightly more than 2,500 people live in each square mile (1,000 people per sq km) of the island, making it one of the most densely populated parts of the world.

In Indonesia, the number of people living in cities and in the countryside is about even. But the percentage of people in the cities has been increasing. In recent years, hundreds of

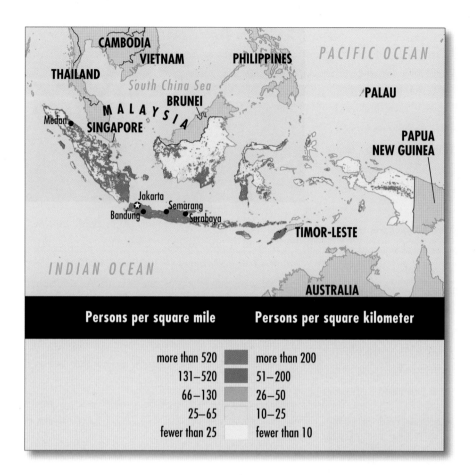

Persons per square mile	Persons per square kilometer
more than 520	more than 200
131–520	51–200
66–130	26–50
25–65	10–25
fewer than 25	fewer than 10

thousands of Indonesians have moved from rural towns and villages to large cities such as Jakarta. They move in search of work and better educational opportunities.

The Language of the Islands

Indonesian is the official language of the nation. It is the primary language used in government affairs, schools, national media, and communication between different ethnic groups. Roughly 17 million people speak Indonesian as their primary language, while as many as 180 million others use it as a

Population of Major Cities (2014 est.)

Jakarta	10,188,000
Surabaya	3,010,000
Bandung	2,560,000
Medan	2,242,000
Semarang	2,067,000

A Diverse People **89**

Transmigrasi: A Movement of People

In 1905, Dutch officials instituted the Transmigration Program, or *transmigrasi* in Indonesian. The goal of the program was to reduce poverty and overcrowding on densely populated islands, such as Java, Bali, and Madura, by moving people to less densely populated areas, such as Papua, Kalimantan, Sumatra, and Sulawesi. The migration also provided a workforce for plantations on Sumatra and helped make the best use of the outer islands' natural resources.

The Dutch moved roughly 650,000 people, mostly from Java to Sumatra's east coast. Many migrants entered into contracts to work on plantations there. If a worker wanted to end the contract, however, the company for which he or she worked often punished him or her with hard labor. Conditions on the plantations were harsh, and the death rate among the workers was very high. Nevertheless, President Sukarno expanded the program after independence in the hopes it would

strengthen Indonesia's economy. At its peak, between 1984 and 1989, roughly 2.5 million people were resettled. In total, between 1905 and 1989, 5 million people were moved to the outer islands. An additional 10 to 15 million people moved to the outer islands independent of the program.

The transmigrasi ultimately failed to improve the migrants' lives or significantly boost the nation's economy. Instead, the program caused serious environmental, social, and political problems. Large tracts of forestland were cleared to create new farmland. However, the soil and climate of the migrants' new homes were usually not as favorable as they had been on Java and Bali. The natural resources of the outer islands became depleted and the land became overgrazed, resulting in soil erosion and deforestation.

The arrival of new residents often caused resentment among the population already living on the outer islands. Violence between the groups flared in many communities. Thousands of people were killed fighting, and many more were made homeless by the conflicts. By the late 1990s, many displaced migrants were fleeing hostilities in Aceh, Kalimantan, Maluku, and other areas. In August 2000, the Indonesian government discontinued the transmigration program.

Common Indonesian Words and Phrases

Halo.	Hello.
Namanya siapa?	What is your name?
Bisa berbahasa Inggris?	Can you speak English?
Terima kasih.	Thank you.
Terima kasih kembali.	You're welcome.
Jam berapa sekarang?	What time is it?
Silakan.	Please.
Ma'af.	I'm sorry.
Selamat pagi.	Good morning.
Selamat malam.	Good night.
Selamat ulang tahun!	Happy birthday!

A mother uses a different form of the Javanese language when she speaks to her daughter than when she speaks to a stranger.

secondary language. The Indonesian alphabet uses the same twenty-six letters as the English alphabet.

More than seven hundred other languages are spoken throughout Indonesia. The most common primary language in Indonesia is Javanese, which is spoken by about eighty-four million people. The Javanese language is spoken in three distinct styles, or levels, depending on the setting, age, and social status of the speakers. Informal speech is used between friends and close relatives, while semiformal is used by strangers meeting for the first time. The formal, polite style is used by young people to address their elders, workers to speak with their bosses, or people of lower status to speak to people of higher status.

CHAPTER 8

Spiritual Life

THE INDONESIAN CONSTITUTION OF 1945 PROCLAIMED, "The state guarantees each and every citizen the freedom of religion and worship in accordance with his religious belief." The constitution added that the state "is based on the belief in the One and Only God." In the mid-1960s, the Indonesian government began a policy requiring each citizen to claim a religion. At the time, Indonesians were required to carry personal identification cards indicating their religion. Today, Indonesia officially recognizes seven religions: Islam, Protestantism, Roman Catholicism, Hinduism, Buddhism, Bahaism, and Confucianism.

Many Indonesians mix these religions with their own local beliefs and practices. Most Indonesians believe that every person has a soul that continues to exist after the body has died. In many Indonesian cultures, there are rituals that help people continue relationships with the souls of their departed relatives.

Opposite: **Muslims pray outside a mosque in Aceh.**

Religions of Indonesia (2010 est.)*	
Islam	87.2%
Protestantism	7.0%
Roman Catholicism	2.9%
Hinduism	1.7%
Other (includes Buddhism and Confucianism)	0.9%
Unspecified	0.4%

*Total does not equal 100% because of rounding.

Islam

Islam is the dominant religion in Indonesia. The religion arrived in Indonesia in the eighth century and had spread throughout the entire archipelago by the fifteenth century. Today, about 87 percent of the population is Muslim. More than two hundred million Indonesians follow Islam, which is the highest Muslim population of any country in the world.

Muslims are guided by the teachings of the Prophet Muhammad, who Muslims believe received messages from God over the course of twenty-two years. These messages are collected into Islam's holy book, called the Qur'an.

Indonesian children at a mosque to study Islam

Muslims in Indonesia generally practice a relaxed form of Islam. Most Indonesians do not pray five times a day. In some areas, Islam is mixed with local traditional customs and religious practices. On Java, for example, these practices sometimes include meditation and requesting assistance from their ancestors. The most conservative form of Islam is practiced in Aceh, in northern Sumatra, the region where Islam was first introduced to Indonesia hundreds of years ago.

Christianity

Together, Protestant and Roman Catholic versions of Christianity are followed by roughly 10 percent of Indonesians. Portuguese and Dutch traders brought Christianity to the islands in the sixteenth and seventeenth centuries. When

People attend Mass in Ende, on the island of Flores. Flores is part of East Nusa Tenggara province, the only province in Indonesia where the majority of people are Catholic.

the Dutch defeated the Portuguese in 1605, they agreed to let Catholicism flourish on Flores and Timor, but expelled the Catholic missionaries from other islands. In place of Catholicism, they established a Protestant church called the Dutch Reformed Church. This denomination remained the dominant Christian group until Indonesia became independent. In the mid-nineteenth century, Protestant Lutherans from Germany began to establish a presence in Indonesia. In the twentieth century, other Protestant missionaries came to the archipelago to spread the faiths. During this time, Catholic and Lutheran churches also experienced strong growth.

In the 1960s, the Indonesian government cracked down on communists and communist supporters, many of whom were atheists—people who do not believe in God. The government insisted that everyone choose a religion. To avoid persecution, many Indonesians adopted Christianity as their religion, and church membership increased substantially.

Today, large numbers of Protestants live in Sumatra, Papua, Maluku, and parts of Sulawesi. Large concentrations of Catholics can be found in Central Java, West Kalimantan, and the eastern part of the Lesser Sunda Islands, most notably on Flores and Timor.

Hinduism

Hinduism arrived in Indonesia with traders and missionaries from India sometime before the second century. Today, Hindus are most common in Indonesia on the island of Bali, where they account for roughly 93 percent of the population. Balinese Hinduism differs from Indian Hinduism in several ways because the Balinese merged Hinduism with their traditional ideas about the world. Balinese Hinduism focuses on local and ancestral spirits, who are thought to be responsible for positive and negative forces that must be kept in balance. Balinese Hindus create beautiful art and rituals to win the

Prambanan: The Hindu Temple

The largest and most spectacular Hindu temple site in Indonesia is located about 11 miles (18 km) northeast of Yogyakarta in central Java. The group of temples is known as the Prambanan Temple Compounds. The first temple on the site was built around 850 to honor Shiva, a Hindu deity. Later kings expanded the compound, but by the 930s, the temples were abandoned and fell into ruin. A major earthquake in the sixteenth century further toppled the neglected structures, and the site was largely forgotten.

Reconstruction of the compound began in 1918, and restoration efforts continue to the present day. Originally, about 240 temples stood in the Prambanan compound. The three principal temples are dedicated

to the three main Hindu forms of god, Shiva, Vishnu, and Brahma. The Shiva temple is the largest, at 154 feet (47 m) tall and 112 feet (34 m) wide. Each of the temples features detailed stone carvings that recount the story of the Hindu religion.

good will of spirits during important events in life, such as birth, death, and marriage.

Buddhism

Buddhism arrived in Indonesia from India and China at roughly the same time, in about the second century CE. It reached its peak in Indonesia between the seventh and fourteenth centuries during the reign of the Srivijaya dynasty. Its popularity decreased after this time, as Islam gained a stronger foothold throughout the archipelago.

Buddhists believe that a person can overcome life's pain and suffering by giving up a desire for worldly objects. Suffering ends when desire ceases and a person reaches a peaceful state of self-fulfillment called enlightenment, or nirvana.

Most Buddhists in Indonesia are of Chinese descent, with the largest presence found in West Kalimantan. Like Muslims, Christians, and Hindus in Indonesia, Buddhists often mix their beliefs with traditional native beliefs and customs.

Religious Holidays

Most of Indonesia's holidays and festivals focus on religious occasions. The most important events in Islam are Ramadan, Eid al-Fitr, and Eid al-Adha. Ramadan is the ninth month of the Islamic calendar. During this time, Muslims fast each day from sunrise to sunset, and take time to reflect on spiritual matters. The fast is broken after sunset each day with a large evening meal, or *iftar*. Eid al-Fitr marks the end of Ramadan. This joyous holiday is celebrated with special foods and delicious sweets, as

A Temple Unearthed

Borobudur, a Buddhist temple in Central Java, is the world's largest Buddhist temple and one of the world's great religious landmarks. Completed in 825 CE, the monument consists of six square platforms topped by three round platforms. Hundreds of stone carvings, many of Buddha—the man on whose teachings Buddhism is based—adorn the huge structure. For hundreds of years, the temple lay buried under layers of volcanic ash, dirt, and jungle growth. In the early nineteenth century, H. C. Cornelius, a Dutch engineer, cleared away the debris to reveal the astounding monument. About 2.5 million people visit Borobudur every year, making it Indonesia's single most visited site.

families gather and friends visit. Eid al-Adha, the feast of the sacrifice, marks the end of the *hajj*, the pilgrimage to Mecca.

A major Hindu celebration in Indonesia is Nyepi, the Day of Silence. This holiday is celebrated mainly in Bali. Nyepi is a day for self-reflection and prayer, in which people do not work, travel, talk, or eat. The day following Nyepi is celebrated as the Balinese New Year's Day.

Waisak is the most important Buddhist holiday. It celebrates the birth, enlightenment, and death of Buddha. Buddhists gather in temples to sing hymns praising Buddha, and often place offerings of flowers and candles at the feet of

Balinese women prepare for Nyepi by bringing offerings of food. This is part of the holiday's ceremonies that are intended to help purify the village.

statues of Buddha. On this holiday, Buddhists give gifts to the aged, the needy, and the sick. Others help decorate temples by painting scenes from the life of Buddha for all worshippers to enjoy and reflect upon.

Among Christians, Easter and Christmas are the most widely celebrated holidays. Christmas celebrations vary greatly across the archipelago. In Jakarta, the community's celebration is called *mandi-mandi*. People gather in the homes of friends and relatives, and draw and paint on each other's faces using white powder. The powder symbolizes atonement and forgiveness for the coming new year. In North Sumatra, Batak communities sacrifice an animal, usually a buffalo or a pig, on Christmas Day. The meat is then divided among the people who purchased the animal.

A monk cleans a Buddha statue at a temple in central Java in preparation for the celebration of Waisak.

CHAPTER 9

Proud Traditions

INDONESIA'S LONG HISTORY HAS GIVEN BIRTH TO A rich culture. Amazing sculptures adorn the nation's historic religious monuments. Museums feature impressive collections of art, textiles, metalwork, jewelry, paintings, and ancient weapons. People tell stories through dance and puppetry and express joy through music. Indonesia's art and culture reveal the creativity of a diverse people with a proud heritage.

Opposite: **Acehnese people perform a traditional dance.**

The Written Word

Indonesia's earliest literature was based on stories passed down from generation to generation by word of mouth. These stories included histories of clans, origin stories, legends, fairy tales, and riddles. As the years passed, Hindu and Muslim stories and poems influenced Indonesian literature. In the twentieth century, the movement for independence stirred literary activity, and the first Indonesian novels were published.

Writer and Nationalist

One of Indonesia's most respected writers was Pramoedya Ananta Toer (1925–2006). Born in Blora in Java, he fought against the Dutch following Sukarno's proclamation of independence on August 17, 1945. During this time, he produced an Indonesian nationalist magazine and worked in radio to promote Indonesia's independence. Angered by his activities, the Dutch arrested Toer. While in prison, he wrote his first major novel, *The Fugitive*.

In the years after independence, Toer wrote a series of novels and short stories about Indonesian society. In his short story collections *Dawn* and *Sparks of Revolution*, he describes the harsh realities of life in the archipelago during the revolution. In *Tales of Bora*, Toer exposes life on Java during the period of Dutch rule.

By the 1960s, Toer supported the Indonesian Communist Party. He was critical of the government, accusing it of ignoring the needs of common Indonesians. When Suharto cracked down on communists in the mid-1960s, Toer was arrested, beaten, and imprisoned.

Although banned from writing, Toer still had many stories to tell. He narrated his thoughts to fellow inmates, who carefully wrote down his words as he spoke. In this way, Toer produced four historical novels that further depicted the hardships under Dutch colonial rule in the twentieth century. Toer was finally released from prison in 1979, but kept under house arrest until 1992. Despite his many years of persecution, Toer had become Indonesia's most acclaimed novelist.

Between the late 1940s and the mid-1960s, many writers expressed revolutionary attitudes that angered government officials. In 1965, novelist Pramoedya Ananta Toer was jailed for his harsh criticism of the Suharto regime. Mochtar Lubis was another writer imprisoned for his outspoken opinions of Indonesia's political leaders. Lubis founded numerous magazines and the newspaper *Indonesia Raya*, and was a powerful advocate for freedom of the press in Indonesia.

Chairil Anwar is best remembered for his poem "Aku" ("Me"), in which he expressed his desire to control his own destiny, rather than be shaped by outside influences. Written in 1943, the poem became a rallying cry for many Indonesians in

The National Museum

Nicknamed the Elephant Museum for its huge bronze elephant statue in the courtyard, the National Museum

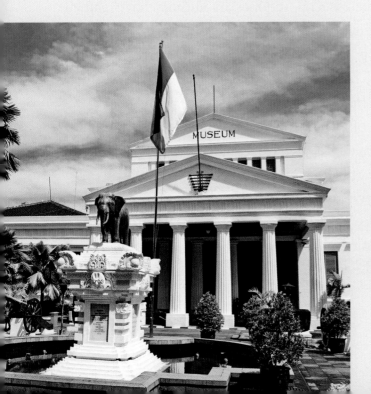

of Indonesia is the nation's leading archaeological and historical museum. Located in Central Jakarta, the museum was built by the Dutch East Indies government and was opened to the public in 1868. An ultramodern addition opened in 2007.

The museum's collection—more than 140,000 artifacts gathered from throughout Indonesia and elsewhere in Asia—traces the history of the region from prehistoric times to the present. It includes the world's largest collection of Hindu and Buddhist art of ancient Indonesia. The collection includes delicately carved statues, ceramics, coins, textiles, and items made of gold and bronze. One of the museum's most popular attractions is its collection of Stone Age artifacts, including fossils of early humans, stone tools, weapons, and ancient drums.

Ayu Utami began her career as a journalist, but after protesting the actions of the Suharto government, she could no longer find work. She turned to fiction and now writes books that explore love, politics, and religion.

their struggle for freedom. The poem includes the lines, "Even if bullets pierce my skin/I will still strike and attack./Wounds and poison I'll take running/Running until the pain leaves."

In recent years, several Indonesian authors have gained international attention. Seno Gumira Ajidarma is a popular writer of fiction, poetry, essays, and films. His works focus on everyday life and true events in Indonesian society. In *Jazz, Perfume and the Incident* (1996), Ajidarma wrote about the bloody massacre of pro-independence demonstrators in East Timor by Indonesian troops. Ayu Utami won critical acclaim for her novel *Saman* (1998), which reflected both on women in a changing society and on Suharto's authoritarianism. Writer and songwriter Dewi Lestari has written about spirituality, religion, and environmentalism in her short stories, novels, and songs. Several of Lestari's works have been adapted into films.

The Joys of Music

Music plays an important role in the Indonesian culture. Many unique instruments have developed in different parts of the country. The *sasando* comes from Rote, one of the Lesser Sunda Islands. It is made of a bamboo tube, palm leaves, and either twenty-eight or fifty-six strings, which the musician plucks.

Gamelan music is the nation's most prominent traditional musical style. A gamelan orchestra features gongs and other metallic instruments. It may include as few as five instruments, or as many as eighty. A full orchestra features a combination of drums, xylophones, gongs, and stringed instruments. Gamelan is played to accompany dance, theater, and special festivities,

Xylophones are common instruments in gamelan orchestras.

such as royal or religious events. Over the years, several varieties of gamelan have developed. Balinese gamelan features brisk, energetic changes of tempo, while Javanese gamelan is known for a slower, more regal style. Gamelan instruments are typically manufactured by local wood- and metalworkers.

Other types of music heard in Indonesia are *tembang sunda*, *dangdut*, and *jaipongan*. Tembang sunda developed during the Dutch colonial period in the mid-nineteenth century. The music, often accompanying poetry recitals, is played on zithers, bamboo flutes, and violins. Modern dangdut is a blend of Middle Eastern pop music, hip-hop, Western rock, and Indian music. The music

A dangdut singer performs in Jakarta. The style got its name from the sound of a drum called the tabla.

Traditional Balinese dance features elaborate costumes and stylized movements.

is played on drums, flutes, mandolins, electric guitars, and synthesizers. Jaipongan is dance music that originated in Western Java in the late 1960s. It typically uses gongs, xylophones, drums, shouting, and a bowed string instrument called a *rebab*.

Dance

Some dances in Indonesia originated as important religious and cultural rituals. The dances were performed to mark a successful harvest, request victory in battle, call for rain, or celebrate certain rites of life, such as birth and death.

Most traditional Indonesian dances tell a story. Well-known dances of Java and Bali, for example, are based on Hindu and Buddhist stories. Classical Javanese dance features slow movements and graceful poses, performed with great control and refinement. Balinese dance is dynamic and energetic. In a type of dance called *barong*, elaborately dressed dancers act out the story of a young woman battling an older witch who is jealous of her youthful vitality.

The puppetry tradition in Indonesia dates back at least a thousand years. Shadow puppets are usually made of leather.

The Art of Puppetry

One of Indonesia's greatest performing arts is called *wayang*, the art of puppetry. Many of the wayang performances are based on ancient Hindu texts.

Many types of wayang can be found in Indonesia. *Wayang kulit*, a type of shadow puppetry, features leather puppets whose shadows are cast on a white cotton screen by the light of an oil lamp. In *wayang golek*, wooden puppets are controlled by rods. *Wayang sadat* is a recently developed form of puppetry that teaches the principles of Islam.

Wayang performances are important events in local villages. When a group of performers arrives in a village, entire families gather to watch the show. During the performances—which can go on into the early hours of the morning—viewers chat with their neighbors, go off for a snack, or even take a nap. It is no wonder that these informal, joyous social gatherings are one of Indonesia's main forms of entertainment.

Weaving

Indonesians' creativity and appreciation of beauty can be seen in the exquisite textiles produced throughout the archipelago. Cotton is the most commonly used fabric, with colorful dyes made from plants or minerals found locally.

Highly skilled craftspeople weave, embroider, and dye cloth for a wide variety of decorative and practical uses. Batik fabrics are made by first drawing a design on a fabric with wax. The cloth is then dipped into dyes, which are absorbed into the unwaxed parts of the fabric. After the cloth dries, the wax is scraped away, and the process is repeated over and over using different colors and designs. *Ikat* cloth is made with threads that have been tie-dyed before they are woven. It can take years to create a single piece of ikat because of this

The Beauty of the Keris

Part weapon, part spiritual object, the *keris* dates back to the time when Hinduism came to Indonesia. Some of the earliest depictions of a keris appear in the ninth-century carvings of Borobudur and Prambanan. An object of great beauty, a keris has a wavy blade and jewel-encrusted handle. Traditionally, a keris was believed to have a spirit and magical powers that enabled it to talk, walk, and fly. It was said it could warn its owner of danger by rattling in its sheath. Some keris were said to help prevent fires, floods, and deaths, while others brought good luck and wealth. Years ago, the keris was worn by Javanese aristocrats to show their power and authority. Today, the weapon is worn only in ceremonies.

Proud Traditions **111**

slow, labor-intensive process. *Songket* is a complex process of decorating silk or cotton with gold or silver threads. When completed, the cloth has a vibrant, shimmering quality.

Carving and Jewelry

Indonesian artisans create elaborate works from wood, animal bone, and stone. Many feature animal figures and geometric patterns. In the western part of the archipelago, Balinese artists carve beautiful statues from *paras*, a soft limestone. In the eastern islands, people carve large ritual posts that repre-

An Indonesian man carves a figure from stone.

Grandmaster Utut Adianto

Born in Jakarta, Utut Adianto developed a passion for the game of chess at an early age. In 1977, at the age of twelve, he won the Jakarta junior championship. Five years later, he won the Indonesian national championship. Piling up victory after victory, Adianto was awarded the title of grandmaster—the highest title a chess player can attain—at the age of twenty-one, becoming the youngest Indonesian to earn the title. In 2009, Adianto was elected to the Indonesian legislature, but he had not lost his affection for chess. "Hopefully, with this position," he said, "I can raise chess to a better horizon in Indonesia, and for most people I shall do my utmost to bring them a better life."

sent the unity of the clan or the connection between God, humans, and ancestors.

Bali and Yogyakarta are renowned for their delicate silver jewelry. Gold *mamuli* pendants, worn around the neck or attached to clothing, are made in Sumba in the Lesser Sunda Islands. Some Sumbanese believe mamuli can help them contact ancestors and spirits. The Dayak people in Kalimantan create stunning jewelry made with beads, stones, coral, crystal, and semiprecious stones such as jade and amethyst.

Sports and Games

Many traditional games are popular in the archipelago. On the island of Nias, off the western coast of Sumatra, young men participate in *hombo batu*, or stone jumping. More a rite of passage than a sport, hombo batu was once used to train

The Art of Kite Flying

Layang-layang, or kite flying, is a popular activity for Indonesian children and adults. One type of layang-layang competition features handsomely decorated kites in the shapes of birds, dragons, or fish that are outfitted with pipes or whistles that make musical sounds as the kites soar through the sky. A panel of judges awards points to the kite with the most inventive shape and sounds. In another layang-layang competition, kites made of light bamboo and waxed paper are used in one-on-one kite dogfights. The string attached to the kite is coated with sharp, crushed glass. The object of the game is to slice the string of the opponent's kite, cutting the kite loose. Sometimes children chase the kite that has been cut loose. Whoever finds the loose kite becomes its new owner.

warriors. The object is to jump over a 5-foot-high (1.5 m) stone wall, sometimes while holding a sword. Participants run about 20 yards (18 m) up to the wall, and then jump high into the air, trying to land feetfirst on the opposite side. In ancient times, the walls were covered with spikes and sharp bamboo sticks. Today, visitors marvel at the brave young men wearing ornate traditional costumes who attempt the dangerous leap.

Sepak takraw is played throughout Indonesia. The game resembles volleyball, but players are not allowed to use their hands. Instead, players must keep the ball in the air using only their feet, knees, chest, and head.

The most popular imported sports in Indonesia are badminton and soccer. Indonesia is one of the world's leading badminton-playing nations. Soccer is played on all levels,

from young children to professionals. The Indonesia Super League is the highest professional level in Indonesia. About twenty teams from around the archipelago play in the league. Basketball, cycling, boxing, and martial arts are also popular in Indonesia.

Children enjoy a game of soccer on a field in Jakarta.

Olympic Glory

Badminton debuted at the 1992 Summer Olympic Games. Since then, Indonesians have been among the most dominant competitors. Winning a total of eighteen medals, Indonesia ranks second only to China in Olympic badminton competition. Badminton requires speed, grace, and lightning-quick reflexes. The first Indonesians to capture gold medals were Alan Budikusuma and Susi Susanti in the men's and women's singles events, respectively, at the 1992 games. Indonesians have also won Olympic medals in weight lifting and archery.

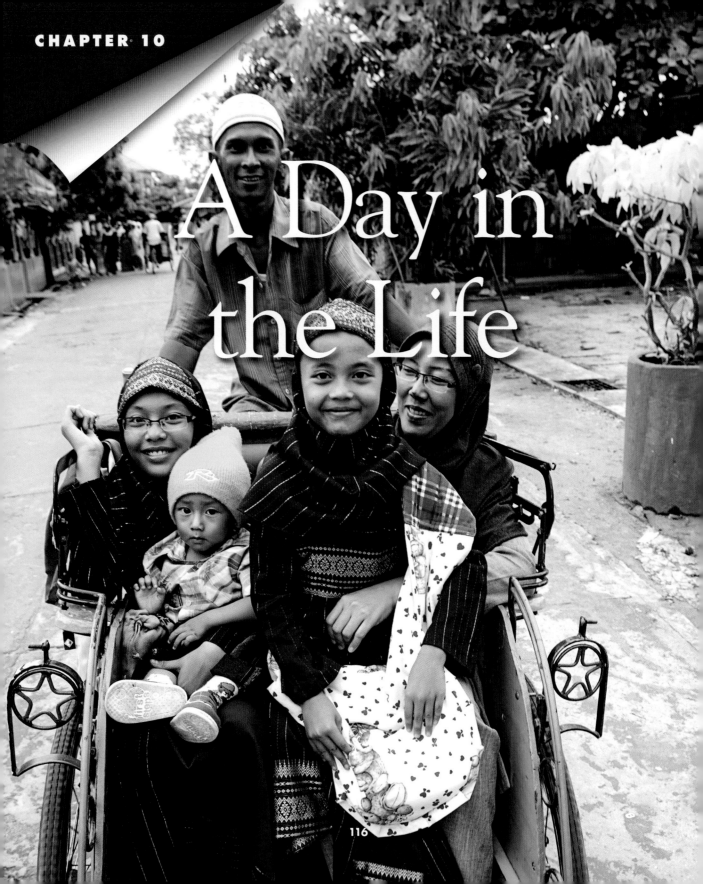

CHAPTER 10

A Day in the Life

116

FAMILY LIFE PLAYS A CENTRAL ROLE IN INDONESIA. The family—including parents, grandparents, aunts, uncles, and cousins—provide support, comfort, and assistance to one another. In families and in larger Indonesian society, showing respect for elders is an important value. In many Indonesian ethnic groups, people also value qualities such as calmness and politeness. People try to hide feelings such as anger and jealousy.

Housing

Tall apartment buildings dot Indonesia's larger cities, such as Jakarta, Surabaya, and Bandung. In recent years, however, the steady influx of people from rural to urban areas has caused a serious housing shortage in large cities. Many people living in densely populated urban neighborhoods often lack electricity, clean water, and adequate health facilities.

Opposite: **A mother takes her children on a ride in a bicycle taxi. Indonesian women have an average of two children.**

Traditional Toraja houses have soaring roofs shaped like saddles.

In rural areas, homes are typically built out of bamboo and other woods, with roofs made of dried palm thatch, tiles, or wood. The floors of houses often consist of earth, concrete, or wooden slats. Many homes are built on stilts. Being high off the ground protects them from floods and heavy rains.

It's in the Bag!

In 2006, the United Nations Children's Fund (UNICEF) launched a program called Art in a Bag in the war-torn province of Aceh. The program's goal was to give elementary school children a way to express their feelings about the violence in their community. Teachers read students Acehnese folktales and encouraged the children to illustrate the stories. Sometimes the students acted out the tales as mini-dramas. Many of the illustrations demonstrated the students' desire for a peaceful and lasting end to the conflict. "We are proud!" said one student. "People from the community and from other schools and even the government came [to see our work]."

Uniforms are required in all Indonesian schools.

Education

Indonesians are required to attend nine years of school. Some attend public schools, while others choose private or semiprivate religious schools, which are usually Islamic. Public schools are divided into three levels: primary (ages six to twelve), junior high (ages twelve to fifteen), and senior high (ages fifteen to eighteen). Only 62 percent of the children in primary school go on to junior high. After junior high, students can attend senior high school or three years of vocational training.

Education in Indonesia is not completely free. Although there is no charge for public schooling at the primary and junior high levels, parents must supply books, paper, writing tools, and uniforms. Many families cannot afford these items. Those children unable to attend school work in the fields or help their families at home. Only the wealthy can afford private schools. A lack of trained teachers, especially in the outer islands, is also a problem.

Indonesia has roughly three thousand schools of higher education, serving more than 4.2 million students. Only 3 percent of the schools are public, however, and tuition costs are high at private universities.

Clothing

Today, most people living in Indonesia's larger cities wear clothes similar to Western-style clothing, including suits, jeans, and T-shirts. At one time, men wore sarongs—large lengths of fabric wrapped around the waist—in the home. Today, sarongs are commonly worn by Muslims when attend-

Boys relax on a beach on the island of Lombok.

The National Costume

The *kebaya*, Indonesia's national costume, was first worn in Indonesia during the fifteenth or sixteenth centuries. The blouse, or kebaya, is usually made from a sheer fabric, such as silk, thin cotton, or a semitransparent polyester or nylon. In Java and Bali, the blouse is cut straight and fits somewhat loosely, while in Sunda it is tight and formfitting. The blouse is often worn over a torso wrap called a *kemben*. The kebaya is usually worn with a *kain*, a 10-foot-long (3 m) piece of fabric tightly wrapped around the waist and legs, and held in place with a string and a belt. Kains are often colorfully dyed and adorned with gold thread, shells, and beads. To keep up with changing times and tastes, modern fashion designers have created kebaya that can be worn with jeans or Western-style dresses.

ing Friday prayers at a mosque. On formal occasions, men often wear batik shirts with trousers or with a *teluk beskap*, a combination of long pants and a sarong. Indonesian women wear the *kebaya*, the national costume of Indonesia, for weddings or formal events. On these occasions, women often drape a long sash called a *selendang* over one shoulder. On less formal occasions, the selendang can be used as a head shawl or to carry babies or objects.

Some remote islands feature more traditional dress. In Papua, the traditional clothing for men and women is a skirt made of dried palm leaves or coconut fiber. Bird feathers are used as accessories for bracelets and necklaces. Papuans often paint their faces and bodies in bright colors with pigments made from plants and animal bone.

National Holidays

New Year's Day	January 1
Chinese New Year	January or February
Good Friday	March or April
Nyepi (Day of Silence, the Balinese New Year)	March
Labor Day	May 1
Waisak (Buddha's birthday)	May or June
Ascension Day of Jesus Christ	May or June
Indonesian Independence Day	August 17
Christmas Day	December 25

In addition, several Muslim holidays are also national holidays. Because the Islamic calendar is eleven days shorter than the Western calendar, when these holidays fall in the Western calendar varies from year to year.

- Islamic New Year
- Birth of the Prophet Muhammad
- Ascension of the Prophet Muhammad
- Eid al-Fitr
- Eid al-Adha

Festivals

In addition to national holidays such as Indonesian Independence Day, Eid al-Fitr, and Christmas, Indonesians celebrate many other festivals. The Bali Arts Festival is a month-long celebration of Balinese music, dance, drama, crafts, and art. It is held each year in Denpasar, the capital of Bali. The festival begins with a huge parade, featuring colorful gamelan orchestras and people dressed in their regional clothing. Hundreds of performers and craftspeople delight audiences each day from morning to late in the evening.

Karapan Sapi, the Bull Races of Madura, attracts thousands of visitors each September and October in search of excitement, good food and music, and speed. The spectacle begins early in the morning, as crowds gather along the street leading to the arena. The bulls, adorned with colorful flowers, ribbons, and headdresses, are paraded through the streets, accompanied by drum and flute bands. When the races begin, the bulls bolt down a 110-yard (100 m) track at speeds topping 30 miles per hour (48 kph), pulling their jockeys on wooden sleds behind them.

A boy speeds down the track during the bull races at Madura.

Let's Eat!

Indonesian cuisine reflects the many different cultures that shaped the nation's history and traditions. Favorite dishes reveal the influence of many lands, including India, China, the Middle East, Japan, Thailand, and the Netherlands.

Rice is the staple food throughout most of Indonesia. It is eaten for breakfast, lunch, and dinner, often served with meat, fish, eggs, or vegetables. Favorite rice dishes include *nasi uduk*, rice cooked in coconut milk; *lontong*, rice steamed in banana leaves; and *nasi goreng*, fried rice. Corn, cassava, and sweet potatoes are the staple foods of the eastern islands.

Nasi goreng is served with many other foods, including eggs and shrimp.

Indonesian Salad Dressing

This tasty dressing can be used to spice up salads or cooked vegetables. It's delicious and easy to make! Have an adult help you.

Ingredients

3 cloves garlic, minced

4 tablespoons oil

3 tablespoons soy sauce

1 tablespoon ginger, finely chopped

2 tablespoons coconut milk

2 tablespoons roasted peanuts, crushed

1 teaspoon lemon juice

½ teaspoon sugar

Pinch of crushed red pepper flakes

Directions

In a large bowl, stir all the ingredients together until thoroughly mixed. Gently pour on salad or cooked vegetables at room temperature or chilled. Enjoy!

A woman arranges smoked fish for sale at a market in the Maluku Islands.

Chicken, beef, goat, pig, and fish are common meats in the Indonesian diet. Chicken is typically fried, grilled, cooked in coconut milk, or put in soup. Roast pig is a popular dish in Bali, North Sumatra, and Papua. Pig meat is often made into *dendeng celeng*, a dried jerky. In more remote areas, such as in the Lesser Sunda Islands, people hunt deer, turtles, snakes, lizards, and fruit bats to eat as part of their diet.

Seafood is abundant in Indonesia, especially in coastal areas. Popular catches include tuna, mackerel, red snapper, swordfish, squid, crabs, and mussels. *Ikan bakar* is a tasty dish made with fish marinated in sweet soy sauce, coconut oil, and spices, and then grilled.

A wide variety of fruit is grown in Indonesia, including bananas, watermelons, papayas, mangoes, and guavas. Some fruits less common in North America are also grown.

Rambutan is a sweet fruit with a white or pinkish jellylike flesh. It is named for its hairy red spines (*rambut* means "hairs"). Some *belimbing*, also called star fruit, are sour and are eaten as pickles or used in relishes. Others are sweet.

Many Indonesians enjoy treats served by street vendors who push their food carts up and down the narrow sidewalks of Indonesia. To attract customers, they bang on brass bells or beat on wooden blocks. Indonesians also eat at *warungs*, which are similar to snack bars, offering customers a place to enjoy a beverage or quickly prepared meal. Many people sit in a warung simply to pass time with friends and acquaintances.

Many traditional Indonesian dishes are available at warungs.

Timeline

INDONESIAN HISTORY		WORLD HISTORY	
Modern humans migrate to what is now Indonesia.	ca. 70,000 years ago		
Migrants from Southeast Asia introduce wet-rice cultivation.	2,500 BCE– 1500 BCE	The Egyptians build the pyramids and the Sphinx in Giza.	ca. 2500 BCE
		The Buddha is born in India.	ca. 563 BCE
Indian traders introduce Hinduism and Buddhism to the Indonesian islands.	ca. 500 CE	The Roman emperor Constantine legalizes Christianity.	313 CE
The Srivijaya Buddhist kingdom on Sumatra establishes trade networks throughout the Indian Ocean.	600s	The Prophet Muhammad begins preaching a new religion called Islam.	610
Arab traders begin spreading Islam in Indonesia.	700s		
The Sailendra kingdom finishes building the Borobudur Buddhist temple in Java.	825	The Eastern (Orthodox) and Western (Roman Catholic) Churches break apart.	1054
		The Crusades begin.	1095
		King John seals the Magna Carta.	1215
The last great Indonesian Hindu empire, Majapahit, thrives.	1293–1527	The Renaissance begins in Italy.	1300s
		The plague sweeps through Europe.	1347
		Ottoman Turks capture Constantinople, conquering the Byzantine Empire.	1453
		Columbus arrives in North America.	1492
The first Dutch expedition arrives in Indonesia.	1596	Reformers break away from the Catholic Church, and Protestantism is born.	1500s
The Dutch gain control of Java.	Early 1600s		
		The U.S. Declaration of Independence is signed.	1776
Indonesia becomes a Dutch colony called the Dutch East Indies.	1799	The French Revolution begins.	1789

INDONESIAN HISTORY

Indonesians fight the Java War against the Dutch.	**1825–1830**
Krakatoa volcano erupts, killing more than 100,000 people and affecting the climate around the world.	**1883**
Sukarno founds the Indonesian Nationalist Party to fight Dutch rule.	**1928**
Japan occupies Indonesia.	**1941–1945**
Indonesia declares its independence; a war with the Dutch begins; Sukarno becomes president.	**1945**
The Dutch give up control of Indonesia.	**1949**
An attempted coup against Sukarno is defeated.	**1965**
At least 300,000 communists are killed.	**1965–1966**
Sukarno resigns; Suharto assumes leadership.	**1967**
Indonesia invades and annexes East Timor.	**1975**
Indonesia's economy suffers during an Asian monetary crisis.	**1997–1998**
Suharto resigns amid protests and riots.	**1998**
Free elections are held in Indonesia for the first time in forty years.	**1999**
East Timor becomes the independent nation of Timor-Leste.	**2002**
A powerful tsunami strikes eleven Indian Ocean nations, killing 220,000 people in Indonesia alone.	**2004**
The Indonesian government and separatists in Aceh agree to a cease-fire.	**2005**
Joko Widodo is elected president.	**2014**

WORLD HISTORY

1865	The American Civil War ends.
1879	The first practical lightbulb is invented.
1914	World War I begins.
1917	The Bolshevik Revolution brings communism to Russia.
1929	A worldwide economic depression begins.
1939	World War II begins.
1945	World War II ends.
1969	Humans land on the Moon.
1975	The Vietnam War ends.
1989	The Berlin Wall is torn down as communism crumbles in Eastern Europe.
1991	The Soviet Union breaks into separate states.
2001	Terrorists attack the World Trade Center in New York City and the Pentagon near Washington, D.C.
2004	A tsunami in the Indian Ocean destroys coastlines in Africa, India, and Southeast Asia.
2008	The United States elects its first African American president.

Fast Facts

Official name: Republic of Indonesia

Capital: Jakarta

Official language: Indonesian

Surabaya

National flag

Year of founding:	1945
National anthem:	"Indonesia Raya" ("Great Indonesia")
Type of government:	Republic
Head of state:	President
Head of government:	President
Area of country:	735,358 square miles (1,904,569 sq km)
Latitude and longitude of geographic center:	5°00' S, 120°00' E
Bordering countries:	East Timor, Malaysia, Papua New Guinea
Highest elevation:	Jaya Peak, 16,024 feet (4,884 m) above sea level
Lowest elevation:	Sea level along the coast
Average high temperature:	In Jakarta, 89°F (32°C)
Average low temperature:	In Jakarta, 77°F (25°C)
Average annual rainfall:	40 to 125 inches (100 to 320 cm) in the lowlands; 240 inches (610 cm) in some mountain areas

Kapuas River

Komodo National Park

Currency

National population (2014 est.):	253,609,643	
Population of major cities (2014 est.):	Jakarta	10,188,000
	Surabaya	3,010,000
	Bandung	2,560,000
	Medan	2,242,000
	Semarang	2,067,000

Landmarks:
- ▶ *Borobudur*, Java
- ▶ *Komodo National Park*, Lesser Sunda Islands
- ▶ *National Museum of Indonesia*, Jakarta
- ▶ *Prambanan Temple Compound*s, Java
- ▶ *Tanjung Puting National Park*, Borneo

Economy: Manufacturing is the largest segment of the Indonesian economy. The country produces chemicals, food products, automobiles, textiles, furniture, and electronics. Indonesia is the largest producer of oil and natural gas in Southeast Asia. Tin, copper, and gold are also mined. The country's major crops include rice, cassava, peanuts, and coffee. Tourism is an important part of Indonesia's economy, with more than eight million visitors entering the country each year.

Currency: The rupiah. In 2014, 12,200 rupiahs equaled US$1.

System of weights and measures: Metric system

Literacy rate: 93%

Students

Pramoedya Ananta Toer

Common Indonesian words and phrases:

Halo.	Hello.
Namanya siapa?	What is your name?
Terima kasih.	Thank you.
Terima kasih kembali.	You're welcome.
Jam berapa sekarang?	What time is it?
Silakan.	Please.
Ma'af.	I'm sorry.
Selamat pagi.	Good morning.
Selamat malam.	Good night.
Selamat ulang tahun!	Happy birthday!

Prominent Indonesians:

Chairil Anwar (1922–1949)
Poet

Diponegoro (1785–1855)
Rebel leader against the Dutch

Raden Adjeng Kartini (1879–1904)
Pioneer for women's rights

Suharto (1921–2008)
Second president

Sukarno (1901–1970)
First president

Susi Susanti (1971–)
Olympic badminton champion

Pramoedya Ananta Toer (1925–2006)
Writer

To Find Out More

Books

- Benoit, Peter. *The Krakatau Eruption.* New York: Children's Press, 2011.

- Bjorklund, Ruth. *Komodo Dragons.* New York: Children's Press, 2012.

- Hibbs, Linda. *All About Indonesia: Stories, Songs and Crafts for Kids.* North Clarendon, VT: Tuttle Publishing, 2014.

- Mirpuri, Gouri, Robert Cooper, and Michael Spilling. *Indonesia.* New York: Marshall Cavendish Benchmark, 2012.

DVDs

- *Cities of the World: Bali.* TravelVideoStore.com, 2009.

- *Cities of the World: Indonesia.* TravelVideoStore.com, 2011.

- *Diving in Bali.* Bubble Vision, 2013.

- *My House Indonesia.* New Dimensions Media, 2011.

▶ Visit this Scholastic Web site for more information on Indonesia:
www.factsfornow.scholastic.com
Enter the keyword **Indonesia**

Index

Page numbers in *italics* indicate illustrations.

Meet the Author

NEL YOMTOV IS AN AWARD-WINNING WRITER AND editor with a passion for writing nonfiction books for young people. In recent years, he has written books about history and geography as well as graphic-novel adaptations of classic mythology, sports biographies, and science topics.

Yomtov was born in New York City. After graduating college, he worked at Marvel Comics, where he handled all phases of comic book production work. Yomtov has also written, edited, and colored hundreds of Marvel comic books. He has served as editorial director of a children's nonfiction book publisher and also as publisher of the Hammond World Atlas book division. In between, he squeezed in a two-year stint as consultant to Major League Baseball, where he helped supervise an educational program for elementary and middle schools throughout the country.

Yomtov lives in the New York area with his wife, Nancy, a teacher and writer, and son, Jess, a sports journalist.

Photo Credits

Photographs ©:

cover: Travel Pictures/Alamy Images; back cover: Angelo Cavalli/Alamy Images; 2: Iryna Rasko/Shutterstock, Inc.; 5: Gregory Adams/Getty Images; 6 left: Dennis Walton/Getty Images; 6 center: James Morga/Getty Images; 6 right: Darren Whiteside/Reuters/Corbis Images; 7 top right: Thomas Cockrem/Alamy Images; 7 top left: AFP/Getty Images; 8: xPacifica/The Image Works; 10: Konrad Wothe/Alamy Images; 12: nik wheeler/Alamy Images; 13: Bloomberg/Getty Images; 14: James Morga/Getty Images; 16: Mark Eveleigh/Alamy Images; 17: Hemis/Alamy Images; 18 top: S009/Getty Images; 18 bottom: Dita Alangkara/AP Images; 19: Ivan Nesterov/Alamy Images; 20: Jason Edwards/Getty Images; 21 top: AGF Srl/Alamy Images; 21 bottom: Sabena Jane Blackbird/Alamy Images; 22: Barry Kusuma/Getty Images; 23: Paul John Fearn/Alamy Images; 25 top: Astronomical Society/Science Source; 25 bottom: Media Bakery; 26: Richard Roscoe/Stocktrek Images/Getty Images; 27: Dita Alangkara/AP Images; 28: age fotostock Spain, S.L./Alamy Images; 30: Boaz Yunior Wibowo/Dreamstime; 31: FLPA/Alamy Images; 32: Dikkyoesin/Dreamstime; 33: K Wothe/Alamy Images; 34: A & J Visage/Alamy Images; 35: Dirscherl Reinhard/Alamy Images; 36: Ethan Daniels/Water/Alamy Images; 37: A & J Visage/Alamy Images; 38: Greenshoots Communications/Alamy Images; 39: blickwinkel/Alamy Images; 40: JTB Media Creation, Inc./Alamy Images; 43: Ivan Vdovin/Alamy Images; 45: The Granger Collection; 47: DEA Picture Library/Getty Images; 48: Interfoto/Alamy Images; 49: Alinari Archives/Getty Images; 51 top: Terrence Spencer/Getty Images; 51 bottom: AP Images; 52: John Florea/Getty Images; 53: AP Images; 54: Reuters/Reuters; 55: Agus Sutedjo/Getty Images; 56 top: Penny Tweedie/Alamy Images; 56 bottom: Choo Youn-Kong/Getty Images; 58: Agencja Fotograficzna Caro/Alamy Images; 60: Jelle vanderwolf//Alamy Images; 61 top: Anupong Boonma/Shutterstock, Inc.; 61 bottom: Tatan Syuflana/AP Images; 63: epa european pressphoto agency b.v./Alamy Images; 64: Darren Whiteside/Reuters/Corbis Images; 65: Romeo Gacad/Getty Images; 66: Achmad Ibrahim/AP Images; 67: Raga Jose Fuste/Alamy Images; 68: Dennis Walton/Getty Images; 70: Qyuplicyter/Thinkstock; 73: Ulet Ifansasti/Getty Images; 74: Sean Sprague/Alamy Images; 76: Tibor Bognar/Alamy Images; 77: Charles O. Cecil/Alamy Images; 78: Peter Ptschelin/Getty Images; 80: Zuma Press, Inc./Alamy Images; 81: Reuters/Reuters; 82: Hotli Simanjuntak/epa/Corbis Images; 83: Peter Horree/Alamy Images; 84: Jenna Addesso; 85 top: AGF Srl/Alamy Images; 85 bottom: Robert Harding World Imagery/Alamy Images; 86: Universal Images Group/DeAgostini/Alamy Images; 87: age fotostock Spain, S.L./Alamy Images; 88: Xinhua/Alamy Images; 90 top: adrian arbib/Alamy Images; 90 bottom: Auscape/UIG/Getty Images; 91: Danita Delimont/Alamy Images; 92: epa european pressphoto agency b.v./Alamy Images; 94: Jorge Fernandez/Alamy Images; 95: Amr Nabil/AP Images; 96: Thomas Cockrem/Alamy Images; 97: Wilmar Photography/Alamy Images; 98: Ron Dahlquist/Media Bakery; 99: AFP/Getty Images; 100: Beawiharta Beawiharta/Reuters; 101: Zuma Press, Inc./Alamy Images; 102: epa european pressphoto agency b.v./Alamy Images; 104: Suzanne Plunkett/AP Images; 105: Prisma Bildagentur AG/Alamy Images; 106: Ulf Andersen/Getty Images; 107: Sylvain Grandadam/Getty Images; 108: AFP/Getty Images; 109: Jenna Addesso; 110: paul kennedy/Alamy Images; 111: Agung Parameswara/Getty Images; 112: Koes Karnadi/Getty Images; 113: Muchtar Zakaria/AP Images; 114: Yadid Levy/Alamy Images; 115: age fotostock Spain, S.L./Alamy Images; 116: Thomas Cockrem/Alamy Images; 118: Hemis/Alamy Images; 119: Art Directors & TRIP/Alamy Images; 120: imageBroker/Alamy Images; 121: Craig Lovell/Eagle Visions Photography/Alamy Images; 122: Darren Whiteside/Reuters; 123: Sijori Images/Barcroft Media/Landov; 124: HLPhoto/Shutterstock, Inc.; 125: Bon Appetit/Alamy Images; 126: Dita Alangkara/AP Images; 127: age fotostock Spain, S.L./Alamy Images; 130: AGF Srl/Alamy Images; 131 top: Anupong Boonma/Shutterstock, Inc.; 131 bottom: Mark Eveleigh/Alamy Images; 132 top: Dirscherl Reinhard/Alamy Images; 132 bottom: Qyuplicyter/Thinkstock; 133 top: Art Directors & TRIP/Alamy Images; 133 bottom: Suzanne Plunkett/AP Images.

Maps by XNR Productions, Inc.